BATTLE HONOURS

THE BATTLE HONOURS OF THE SECOND WORLD WAR

1939 – 1945

and

KOREA

1950 – 1953

[British and Colonial Regiments]

Compiled from Official Records

Revised and corrected by Colonel Terry Cave

2003

Published by
The Naval & Military Press Ltd
Unit 10 Ridgewood Industrial Park,
Uckfield, East Sussex,
TN22 5QE England
Tel: +44 (0) 1825 749494
Fax: +44 (0) 1825 765701
www.naval-military-press.com

© *The Naval & Military Press Ltd 2003*

CONTENTS

Preface	i
Introduction	iii
Second World War, 1939 – 45	
Norway, 1940-41	1
North-West Europe, 1940, '42, '44-45	3
Abyssinia, 1940-41	42
British Somaliland, 1940	52
Iraq, 1941	53
Syria, 1941	54
North Africa, 1940-43	56
Sicily, 1943	93
Italy, 1943-45	98
Greece, 1941 and 1944-45	137
Middle East, 1941-45	139
Malta, 1940-42	142
Malaya, 1941-42	143
South-East Asia, 1941	146
Burma, 1942-45	147
Honorary Distinctions	170
Korea, 1950-53	172
Index to Battle Honours	176

PREFACE

In 1925 the War Office published an Army Order listing all the Battle Honours awarded to regiments of the British Army indicating which had been selected to be borne on the Colours or Appointments. This was the final list apart from three late applications and some minor amendments. In 1958 the War Office published a Record of all Battle Honours awarded to British (including British Gurkha) Regiments and Colonial Regiments for World War II and the Korean War, Regiments of the Commonwealth were not included. This is that list. The addressees shown at the end of the **Introduction** indicate a very limited distribution.

When this record was being checked prior to publication by the Naval & Military Press it quickly became clear there were many errors, typographical, grammatical and factual. To begin with quite a few new regiments put in an appearance and here are some examples: The Highland<u>ers</u> Light Infantry (very popular), The King's Own Yeomanry Light Infantry, The K.A.R.R.R.C (an amalgamation of the King's African Rifles with the King's Royal Rifle Corps?), The London Irish Fusiliers, The London Irish Buffs and The Royal West King Regiment. There were also cases where Honours not elected to be borne on the Colours were shown as elected and vice versa.

With each action designated as a Battle Honour there is a brief summary of the operation, sometimes naming units involved. This description was left except in cases where there were mistakes in Order of Battle details or where the write up was confusing. Another source of confusion was the designation of Indian Army units, such as the 12th Frontier Force Regiment and the 13th Frontier Force Rifles, two different regiments. There were problems with spelling of place names, for example St Pierre Lancers Vielle, a highly unusual rendering of St Pierre La Vieille, Sidi Rezech for Sidi Rezegh, Gameela for Gambela and Agrodat for Agordat. Finally there was the index which contained many names that had nothing to do with anything, these were rigorously pruned and the names that remain are those for which Battle Honours were awarded.

The following published works were used for reference:

The Battle Honours of the British and Indian Armies 1662-1982 H.C.B Cook. The most important book on its subject and a magnificent piece of work. For some reason he omits The Tower Hamlets Rifles in his WWII regiments. A descendant of the WWI London Regiment, it had three battalions at one time during WWII

Orders of Battle Second World War 1939-1945 Lieut-Col H.F. Joslen

Commonwealth Divisions 1939-1945 Malcolm A. Bellis

Regiments and Corps of the British Army Ian S. Hallows

Handbook of British Regiments Christopher Chant

A Register of the Regiments and Corps of the British Army edited by Arthur Swinson.

Terry Cave
Worthing, July 2003

INTRODUCTION

The object of this Record is to provide a means of quick reference to those Battles, Actions and Engagements of the Second World War, which were awarded as Honours to the Regiments represented at them. Although in most cases a brief summary of the operation is made, with an indication of the troops involved, the background to the story must be read in the Official Histories, or Divisional or other Histories, which will provide a fuller account. Moreover, while the Army List will show all the Honours awarded to one regiment, this Record will make clear all the British Regiments to whom any one award has been made.

Regiments are shown by the names under which they won the award.

This Record covers only the British Regiments involved for whom awards were recommended by the War Office Battle Honours Committee. In many cases, (as will be seen from the outline orders of Battle indicated in the summaries) other Commonwealth troops were concerned. Awards in their cases are a matter for arrangement direct between the Commonwealth Government concerned and the Sovereign, and these awards are not made known officially to the War Office.

The Official List of Battles, Actions and Engagements as drawn up by the Battles Nomenclature Committee in their First Report, contains 970 classified operations, exclusive of these which took place in the South and South-West Pacific (which did not involve any British fighting units), which are included in the Final Report by the R.N.C. 633 of these operations are listed in this Record, and it will be appreciated that many of the remainder exclusively concern Commonwealth Forces. For this reason, or because the qualifying rules for Honours did not permit of an award, there are several gaps in the sequence of serials in the Official List compared with the Awards listed.

The official classification of each operation in the Official List has been indicated in the summaries which follow by reference to 'subsidiary Action' (or 'Engagement') when the serial refers to an operation with a 'Battle.' Where Actions or Engagements, however, were separate, they are so indicated by the use of a capital A or E.

The sequence of the Official List has been followed throughout. This is generally chronological, by Theatres, but not always so, as the campaigns are divided into 'Phases'. These Phases will be found in the Official List.

It may be of interest to summarise the Battles in the Second World War for which the largest number of awards were made. As a general rule, this indicates those Battles in which the greatest number of different units were employed.

Awards to 20 or more Regiments were made as follows (figures in brackets represent the number emblazoned in each case):-

40 Regiments and over

1. Rhine   49 (36)
2. El Alamein   43 (42)
3. Rhineland   43 (19)
4. Mont Pincon   42 (16)

30 Regiments and over

5.	Caen	37	(22)
6.	Nederrijn	35	(6)
7.	Odon	33	(17)
8.	Tunis	32	(19)
9.	Gothic Line	31	(16)
10.	Normandy Landing	29	(29)
11.	Anzio	29	(24)
12.	Falaise	30	(13)

20 Regiments and over

13.	Argenta Gap	29	(16)
14.	Cassino II	24	(23)
15.	Gazala	26	(13)
16.	North Arakan	23	(13)
17.	Bourguebus Ridge	23	(9)
18.	Coriano	23	(8)
19.	St Omer-La Bassee	23	(8)
20.	Tobruk, 1941	22	(12)
21.	Landing in Sicily	21	(8)
22.	Garigliano Crossing	21	(7)
23.	Advance to Florence	21	(4)

The theatre distribution of the above is:-

North-West Europe	10
Italy	7
North Africa	4
Sicily	1
Burma	1

Also included in this Record is a list of the Honorary Distinctions awarded to regiments or battalions which were converted to fight in an Arm to which Honours are not awarded, and which were subsequently reconverted to their original Arm. In such cases, they would once again be entitled to carry Guidons or Colours, but their war services would have been unrecognised by awards of battle honours. To fill this gap, awards of Honorary Distinctions were made, to indicate the war services rendered.

Finally, the record includes the Honours awarded for the Korean Campaign of 1950-53. The manner of showing these follows the principles outlined above in respect of the Second World War.

Four copies of this Record were made, lodged as follows:-

Copy No 1	War Office Library
Copy No 2	Secretary, Honours and Distinctions Committee, P.S.12, War Office
Copy No 3	P.S.12, War Office
Copy No 4	Cabinet Office Archives, Great George Street

The War Office *Secretary*
31st March, 1958 *Battle Honours Committee, 1954-58*

NORWAY, 1940-41

In April, 1940, in an attempt to forestall a German occupation of Norway, two Anglo-French expeditions were sent to that country. The first, in central Norway, entailed two main landings, in the Namsos area north of Trondheim, and in the Andalsnes area south of Trondheim.

The second expedition, comprising Franco-Polish troops, landed in the Narvik area, while British forces were deployed further south in the Mosjoen-Mo-Bodo area to hold off enemy forces advancing from the south.

The campaign of 1940 was over by the end of May. In the closing days of 1941, a raid at Vaagso was responsible for the addition of that year to the Theatre Honour.

The Theatre Honour of 'Norway, 1940,' was selected to be borne on the Colours of:

> Irish Guards
> The Green Howards (Alexandra, Princess of Wales's Own Yorkshire Regiment)
> The South Wales Borderers
> The Sherwood Foresters (Nottinghamshire and Derbyshire Regiment)
> The King's Own Yorkshire Light Infantry

and has also been awarded to:

> Scots Guards
> The Royal Lincolnshire Regiment
> The Royal Leicestershire Regiment
> The York and Lancaster Regiment.

The Theatre Honour of 'Norway, 1941,' was awarded to the Commando Association.

VIST

21st to 22nd April, 1940

In this Engagement, overwhelming German forces including ski-troops attacked 146th Brigade, using infiltration tactics. British casualties in the area amounted to 157 officers and men killed, missing and wounded.

The Honour has been awarded to:

> The Royal Lincolnshire Regiment.

KVAM   OTTA

25th to 26th April, 1940   28th April, 1940

The 15th and 148th Brigades provided the troops in this area, carrying out the fighting withdrawal during which these Engagements were fought, and in which the British troops lost a quarter of their strength in casualties.

'Kvam' has been awarded to:-

> The King's Own Yorkshire Light Infantry.

'Otta' has been awarded to:-

> The Green Howards (Alexandra, Princess of Wales's Own Yorkshire Regiment).

STIEN
17th May to 18th May, 1940

POTHUS
25th to 26th May, 1940

24th Guards Brigade was the British formation involved in these Engagements in this area, where a withdrawal was again being conducted in the face of enemy attacks.

'Stien' has been awarded to the:-

    Scots Guards.

'Pothus' has been awarded to the:-

    Irish Guards.

VAAGSO
27th December, 1941.

In this Engagement, Nos. 2 and 3 Commandos carried out a successful raid to destroy fish-oil factories and shipping. There was severe fighting on the island of Maaloy and on Vaagso. 150 Germans were killed and 98 captured.

The Honour has been awarded to:-

    The Commando Association.

NORTH-WEST EUROPE, 1940, '42, '44–45

After eight months of operational inactivity, the British Expeditionary Force in France advanced, in May, 1940, to the line of the River Dyle in Belgium to meet the oncoming Germany Armies. The main attack of the latter was made on the 12th May, against the French some 25 miles to the south of the British right flank, with the result that the Channel coast was reached by the 23rd May, the lines of communication of the B.E.F. having been cut by 21st May.

The main body of the B.E.F. began to withdraw on the night 16th/17th May, to be evacuated eventually from Dunkirk by 3rd June.

Parts of two divisions which had been cut off, with L. of C. troops, and other divisions landed in France continued to fight south of the Somme until 18th June, when the 1940 campaign ended.

Raiding operations against the coast of France in 1942 account for the addition of this year to the Theatre Honour.

British Forces landed in France again in the assault on Normandy on the 6th June, 1944, and by May, 1945, their victorious armies stood on the banks of the Elbe and the shores of the Baltic and North Sea.

'North-West Europe, 1940, '44-45,' was selected for emblazonment by the:-

13th/18th Hussars	Gloucestershire Regiment
15th/19th Hussars	Worcestershire Regiment
Royal Tank Regiment	Duke of Cornwall's Light Infantry
Lothians and Border Horse	Duke of Wellington's Regiment
Fife and Forfar Yeo.	South Lancashire Regiment
Coldstream Guards	Essex Regiment
Royal Scots	King's Shropshire Light Infantry
Royal Warwickshire Regiment	King's Royal Rifle Corps
Royal Norfolk Regiment	Highland Light Infantry
East Yorkshire Regiment	Gordon Highlanders
Green Howards	Rifle Brigade
Cameronians	

and has also been awarded to the:-

4th/7th Dragoon Guards	East Lancashire Regiment
5th Dragoon Guards	Royal Hampshire Regiment
East Riding Yeomanry	Black Watch
Grenadier Guards	Oxfordshire and Buckinghamshire Light Infantry
Welsh Guards	Dorset Regiment
Queen's Royal Regiment	Royal Berkshire Regiment
Royal Northumberland Fusiliers	Middlesex Regiment
R. Lincolnshire Regiment	Wiltshire Regiment
Suffolk Regiment	Manchester Regiment
Royal Scots Fusiliers	Yorkshire and Lancaster Regiment
Cheshire Regiment	Durham Light Infantry
Royal Welch Fusiliers	Seaforth Highlanders
King's Own Scottish Borderers	Cameron Highlanders

Kensington Regiment
Argyll and Sutherland Highlanders
Royal Ulster Rifles

'North-West Europe, 1940,' was emblazoned by the:-

9th Lancers
12th Lancers
Buffs
King's Own Royal Regiment
Bedfordshire and Hertfordshire Regiment
Royal Inniskilling Fusiliers
East Surrey Regiment
Royal Sussex Regiment
Royal West Kent Regiment
Queen Victoria's Rifles (T.A.)

and has also been awarded to the:-

Queen's Bays
10th Royal Hussars
Royal Fusiliers
West Yorkshire Regiment
Loyal Regiment
Sherwood Foresters

'North-West Europe, 1940,' 44, was emblazoned by the:-

South Staffordshire Regiment
Border Regiment

and was also awarded to the:-

Lancashire Fusiliers
North Staffordshire Regt.

'North-West Europe, 1940,' 45, was emblazoned by the:-

Northampton Regiment

'North-West Europe, 1942, '44-45', was awarded to the:-

Parachute Regiment
Commando Association

'North-West Europe, 1944' is borne on the Colours of the:-

Hertfordshire Regiment

and has also been awarded to the:-

24th Lancers
King's Regiment

'North-West Europe, 1944-45' was emblazoned by the:-

Life Guards
Royal Horse Guards
1st Royal Dragoons
8th King's Royal Irish Hussars
Sherwood Rangers Yeomanry
Westminster Dragoons
3rd/4th County of London Yeomanry
Inns of Court Regiment
Honourable Artillery Company
Herefordshire Light Infantry
Scots Guards
Irish Guards
Somerset Light Infantry
Royal Leicestershire Regiment
South Wales Borderers
King's Own Yorkshire Light Infantry
Glider Pilot Regiment
Queen's Westminsters
London Rifle Brigade
Special Air Service Regiment

and was also awarded to the:-

4th/7th Dragoon Guards
Royal Scots Greys
11th Hussars
22nd Dragoons
Staffordshire Yeomanry
Derbyshire Yeomanry
Northamptonshire Yeomanry
Devonshire Regiment
Welch Regiment
Monmouthshire Regiment

DYLE

10th to 16th May, 1940

This was the opening Action of the campaign in Belgium. I Corps (1st, 2nd and 48th Divisions) and II Corps (3rd and 4th Divisions) held an area from Wavre to the ferry north of Louvain. Enemy probing attacks were made and repelled until midnight 15th/16th May, when withdrawal took place.

The Honour was emblazoned by the:-

    4th/7th Royal Dragoon Guards   Manchester Regiment
    12th Lancers   North Staffordshire Regiment
    Royal Berkshire Regiment   Royal Ulster Rifles

and has also been awarded to the:-

    13th/18th Hussars   Royal Welch Fusiliers
    Grenadier Guards   Middlesex Regiment
    Coldstream Guards   Durham Light Infantry
    Royal Scots   Cheshire Regiment

WITHDRAWAL TO ESCAUT

17th to 19th May, 1940

This Action commemorates the contact with the enemy along the whole front of withdrawal from the River Dyle on the 18th and 19th May.

The Honour is born on the Standard and Guidon of the:-

    5th Dragoon Guards   15th/19th Hussars

and has been awarded to the:-

    13th/18th Royal Hussars   Cheshire Regiment
    East Riding Yeomanry   Manchester Regiment
    East Yorkshire Regiment   Gordon Highlanders
    Royal Irish Fusiliers

DEFENCE OF ESCAUT

19th to 22nd May, 1940

Throughout 20th and 21st May, the enemy attacked with increasing strength in the endeavour to establish bridgeheads over the river. Partial success was achieved in places, and this Action commemorates some hard fighting.

The Honour is borne on the Colours of the:-

    Royal Scots   Lancashire Fusiliers
    Royal Warwickshire Regiment   Gloucestershire Regiment

and has also been awarded to the:-

    Coldstream Guards   Border Regiment
    Queen's Royal Regiment   Royal Sussex Regiment
    Royal Northumberland Fusiliers   Oxfordshire and Buckinghamshire Light Infantry
    Buffs   Northamptonshire Regiment
    Royal Norfolk Regiment   Royal West Kent Regiment

East Yorkshire Regiment	King's Shropshire Light Infantry
Royal Welch Fusiliers	Middlesex Regiment
Worcestershire Regiment	Manchester Regiment
East Lancashire Regiment	North Staffordshire Regiment
East Surrey Regiment	Cameron Highlanders
Duke of Cornwall's Light Infantry	

AMIENS, 1940

20th May

In this Engagement the Germans attacked 7/R. Sussex in their position astride the Amiens-Poix road, where they suffered heavy casualties.

The Honour has been awarded to the:-

Royal Sussex Regt.

DEFENCE OF ARRAS

19th to 24th May, 1940.

This Engagement commemorates the stand by various formations and units under command of Major-General R. L. Petre, in which some severe fighting occurred.

The Honour is borne on the Colours of the:-

Welsh Guards	Manchester Regiment
Wiltshire Regiment	

and has also been awarded to the:-

12th Lancers	Royal Inniskilling Fusiliers
East Yorkshire Regiment	Black Watch
Green Howards	Northamptonshire Regiment
Royal Scots Fusiliers	

ARRAS COUNTER ATTACK

21st May, 1940

In this Engagement a counter attack was launched from Vimy Ridge with 1st Anti-Tank Brigade, 151st Brigade of 50th Division, and two anti-tank batteries of 5th Division.

The Honour has been awarded to the:-

12th Lancers	Durham Light Infantry
Royal Tank Regiment	
Royal Northumberland Fusiliers	

BOULOGNE, 1940

22nd to 25th May

This Action commemorates the defence of the town by the Irish Guards and Welsh Guards, who bear the Honour on their Colours.

CALAIS, 1940

22nd to 26th May

This Action denotes the gallant defence of the town by the Greenjacket Brigade. The Honour is borne on the Appointments of the:-

    Queen Victoria's Rifles   King's Royal Rifle Corps
    Rifle Brigade

and has also been awarded to the Royal Tank Regiment.

FRENCH FRONTIER, 1940

23rd to 27th May

Fighting of varying intensity took place in this Action.

    The Honour has been awarded to the:-   East Yorkshire Regiment

ST. OMER-LA BASSEE

23rd to 29th May, 1940

In this Battle, the bigger of the two recorded for the 1940 campaign, some bitter fighting occurred over a widespread area. The success of the ultimate evacuation from Dunkirk largely depended on the fighting both in this and the Battle of the Ypres-Comines Canal.

The Honour was emblazoned by the:-

5th Dragoon Guards	Cheshire Regiment
East Riding Yeomanry	Dorset Regiment
Royal Norfolk Regiment	Cameron Highlanders
Royal Irish Fusiliers	Royal Welch Fusiliers

and has also been awarded to the:-

Royal Tank Regiment	Royal Sussex Regiment
Welsh Guards	Essex Regiment
Royal Scots	Sherwood Foresters
Buffs	Royal Berkshire Regiment
King's Own	Manchester Regiment
Royal Northumberland Fusiliers	Durham Light Infantry
Lancashire Fusiliers	Worcestershire Regiment
Gloucestershire Regiment	

WORMHOUDT

28th May, 1940

This subsidiary Engagement covers the scene of fierce resistance by British troops to repeated attacks by the enemy attempting to cut off the British Army.

The Honour is borne on the Colours of the:-

    Royal Warwickshire Regiment

and has also been awarded to the:-

    Cheshire Regiment   Worcestershire Regiment

Gloucestershire Regiment

CASSEL
27th to 29th May, 1940

Stubborn fighting took place in this subsidiary Engagement, in which 48th Division held off fierce attacks by enemy armour, until finally the town was surrounded and the gallant garrison had to fight its way out.

This Honour was emblazoned by the:-

    East Riding Yeomanry   Oxfordshire and Buckinghamshire Light Infantry
    Gloucestershire Regiment

and was also awarded to the:-

    Cheshire Regiment

FORET DE NIEPPE
27th to 28th May, 1940

In this subsidiary Engagement an attempt was made to delay the German advance northwards towards Cassel.

This Honour has been awarded to the:-

    Royal Sussex Regiment   Royal West Kent Regiment

YPRES-COMINES CANAL
26th to 28th May, 1940

In this Battle, 5th Division, under Major-General H. E. Franklyn, was largely instrumental in making time for the embarkation to begin at Dunkirk, by fiercely resisting all German attacks to break through to the coast.

The Honour is borne on the Guidon and Colours of the:-

    13th/18th Hussars   Oxfordshire and Buckinghamshire Light Infantry
    Royal Warwickshire Regiment   North Staffordshire Regiment
    Royal Scots Fusiliers

and has also been awarded to the:-

    East Yorkshire Regiment   Wiltshire Regiment
    Cameronians   Sherwood Foresters
    Royal Inniskilling Fusiliers   Middlesex Regiment
    The Black Watch   Manchester Regiment
    Northamptonshire Regiment   Seaforth Highlanders
    Gordon Highlanders

DUNKIRK, 1940
26th May to 3rd June

The period covering this Action denotes the period of embarkation during which 338,226 troops were evacuated. The Honour has been restricted to those units which actually held and fought on the perimeter during this time, and thus accounts for the absence of many names of regiments who were present but whose fighting in the campaign was already over.

The Honour was accepted for emblazonment by the:-

- 4th/7th Dragoon Guards
- 5th Dragoon Guards
- 12th Lancers
- Fife and Forfar Yeomanry
- Grenadier Guards
- Coldstream Guards
- King's Own
- Royal Northumberland Fusiliers
- Royal Fusiliers
- Royal Lincolnshire Regiment
- Suffolk Regiment
- East Yorkshire Regiment
- Bedfordshire and Hertfordshire Regiment
- Royal Ulster Rifles
- King's Own Scottish Borderers
- East Lancashire Regiment
- Duke of Wellington's Regiment
- East Surrey Regiment
- Border Regiment
- Royal Hampshire Regiment
- South Lancashire Regiment
- Loyal Regiment
- Royal Berkshire Regiment
- King's Shropshire Light Infantry
- Middlesex Regiment
- Durham Light Infantry

and has also been awarded to the:-

- Green Howards
- Cheshire Regiment
- Black Watch
- Sherwood Foresters
- Gordon Highlanders

SOMME, 1940

24th May to 5th June

This Action, in which units of 1st Armoured and 51st Highland Divisions took part, under French command, covers abortive attempts to secure the river crossings.

The Honour is borne on the Colours of the:-

- Queen's Bays
- 9th Lancers
- 10th Hussars

and has also been awarded to the:-

- Royal Tank Regiment
- Lothians and Border Horse
- Royal Scots Fusiliers
- Border Regiment
- Seaforth Highlanders
- Gordon Highlanders
- Cameron Highlanders
- Argyll and Sutherland Highlanders
- Black Watch

WITHDRAWAL TO SEINE

6th to 10th June, 1940

This Action was a fighting withdrawal from the Somme in the face of German attacks.

The Honour has been awarded to the:-

- Queen's Bays
- 9th Lancers
- Lothians and Border Horse
- Buffs
- Royal Scots Fusiliers
- Seaforth Highlanders

WITHDRAWAL TO CHERBOURG
9th to 18th June, 1940

This was the last Engagement of the 1940 campaign, in which the hastily landed troops of 52nd Lowland Division found themselves re-embarking within a few days.

The Honour has been awarded to the:-
- Highland Light Infantry

ST VALERY-EN-CAUX
10th to 12th June, 1940

The name of this Engagement commemorates the disastrous end of the 51st Highland Division in France, having fought gallantly and being finally killed or captured.

The Honour is borne on the Colours of the:-
- Duke of Wellington's Regiment
- Seaforth Highlanders
- Kensington Regiment

and has also been awarded to the:-
- Lothians and Border Horse
- Royal Norfolk Regiment
- Black Watch
- Gordon Highlanders
- Cameron Highlanders

SAAR
13th May, 1940

Early in this month 51st Division took over an extended sector in the Maginot Line.

This Engagement denotes the defeat of a German attack on the British defences.

The Honour is borne on the Colours of the:-
- Kensington Regiment

And has also been awarded to the:-
- Black Watch

BRUNEVAL
27th to 28th February, 1942

This Engagement commemorates a gallant raid on a German radar station, the Honour for which is borne on the Colours of the:-
- Parachute Regiment

ST. NAZAIRE
27th to 28th March, 1942

This successful Engagement, in which a Naval force and No. 2 Commando co-operated, resulted in the blocking of the harbour for use by 'U' Boats.

The Honour was awarded to the:-

Commando Association

DIEPPE

19th August, 1942

In this Action, Nos. 3 and 4 Commandos, with a Royal Marine Commando, took part under command of 2nd Canadian Division in a raid on Dieppe which failed with very heavy casualties.

The Honour was awarded to the:-

Commando Association

NORMANDY LANDING

6th June, 1944

This Battle was the assault landing on and across the Normandy beaches. Under Second Army were I and XXX Corps, with 6th Airborne Division, 3rd Division, 3rd Canadian Division, 50th Division, and 1st and 4th Special Service Brigades. Additionally, 27th Armoured Brigade was under command of 3rd Division; 2nd Canadian Armoured Brigade under 3rd Canadian Division; and 56th Brigade and 8th Armoured Brigade were under 50th Division.

The Honour was emblazoned by the:-

- 4th/7th Dragoon Guards
- 13th/18th Hussars
- 22nd Dragoons
- Sherwood Rangers Yeomanry
- Staffordshire Yeomanry
- Westminster Dragoons
- East Riding Yeomanry
- Inns of Court Regiment
- Royal Warwickshire Regiment
- King's Regiment
- Royal Norfolk Regiment
- Royal Lincolnshire Regiment
- Devonshire Regiment
- Suffolk Regiment
- Hertfordshire Regiment
- East Yorkshire Regiment
- Green Howards
- Cheshire Regiment
- South Wales Borderers
- Royal Hampshire Regiment
- Dorset Regiment
- South Lancashire Regiment
- Oxfordshire and Buckinghamshire Light Infantry
- Royal Berkshire Regiment
- King's Shropshire Light Infantry
- Middlesex Regiment
- Royal Ulster Rifles
- Glider Pilot Regiment
- Parachute Regiment

and was also awarded to the:-

Commando Association

PEGASUS BRIDGE

6th June, 1944

This subsidiary Engagement denotes the capture by coup de main of the Orne bridges.

The Honour was emblazoned by the:-

Oxfordshire and Buckinghamshire Light Infantry   Glider Pilot Regiment

And was also awarded to the:-

Parachute Regiment

MERVILLE BATTERY

6th June, 1944

In this subsidiary Engagement units of 6th Airborne Division captured the Merville Battery.

The Honour was emblazoned by the:-

Glider Pilot Regiment

and was also awarded to the:-

Parachute Regiment

PORT EN BESSIN

7th to 8th June, 1944

This Engagement covers the capture by 50th Division of Port en Bessin and Escures, and the link up with the 1st U.S. Division which joined the British bridgehead with that of the Americans.

The Honour was awarded to the:-

Devonshire Regiment

SULLY

8th to 9th June, 1944

In this Engagement, stiff fighting by 50th Division caused the enemy to withdraw from this strong point.

The Honour was emblazoned by the:-

South Wales Borderers

CAMBES

9th June, 1944

This Engagement was fought by 3rd Division, the village being attacked and captured after some severe fighting.

The Honour was emblazoned by the:-

East Riding Yeomanry

and was also awarded to the:-

Royal Lincolnshire Regiment	Middlesex Regiment
King's Own Scottish Borderers	Royal Ulster Rifles

PUTOT EN BESSIN

8th June, 1944

3rd Canadian Division had stiff fighting with enemy armour in this Engagement, recapturing the village after being forced out of it.

The Honour was emblazoned by the:-

24th Lancers

BREVILLE

10th to 13th June, 1944

In this Engagement a German counter-attack on the eastern flank was defeated, and the flank was secured by the capture of the Breville ridge, during operations conducted by 6th Airborne Division. The fighting included that at Chateau St. Come and Bois de Mont; the enemy attack on Ranville, the counter attack by 7/Parachute Battalion, and the attack on Breville.

The Honour is borne on the Colours of the:-

    Parachute Regiment

and was also awarded to the:-

    13th/18th Hussars   Middlesex Regiment
    Black Watch

VILLERS BOCAGE

8th to 15th June, 1944

This Action, in which 7th Armoured Division and 8th Armoured Brigade Group, with 49th and 50th Divisions, were involved, included the operations to secure Villers Bocage, beginning with the thrust to Audrieu and St. Pierre by 8th Armoured Brigade Group; and the subsequent operations around Tilly sur Seulles with the final withdrawal of 7th Armoured Division.

The Honour was emblazoned by the:-

    8th Hussars   Westminster Dragoons
    11th Hussars   Queen's Royal Regiment
    24th Lancers

and was also awarded to the:-

    Sherwood Rangers Yeomanry   Dorset Regiment
    3rd/4th County of London Yeomanry Durham Light Infantry
    Gloucestershire Regiment   Rifle Brigade

TILLY SUR SEULLES

14th to 19th June, 1944

This 50th Division Engagement covers the operations about Lingevres and Hottot, including the defeat of enemy armoured counter attacks, ending with the capture of Tilly sur Seulles.

The Honour was emblazoned by the:-

    24th Lancers   Durham Light Infantry

and was also awarded to the:-

    Devonshire Regiment   Royal Hampshire Regiment
    East Yorkshire Regiment   Dorset Regiment
    Green Howards   Essex Regiment
    Duke of Wellington's Regiment   Kensington Regiment

ODON

25th June to 2nd July, 1944

The following formations took part in this Battle.

I Corps:	8th Brigade (3rd Division)
VIII Corps:	15th Division, 43rd Division, 11th Armoured Division, 4th Armoured Brigade, 31st Tank Brigade, 32nd Guards Brigade, 160th Brigade (53rd Division).
XXX Corps:	49th Division, 8th Armoured Brigade

The attack was made from west of Caen to encircle the city and secure the high ground of the Bourguebus Ridge. After crossing the River Odon the attack failed to maintain sufficient impetus to carry it across the Orne and came to a standstill on the slopes of Hill 112 in face of determined enemy counter attacks, strong in armour.

The Honour was emblazoned by the:-

4th/7th Dragoon Guards
22nd Dragoons
23rd Hussars
24th Lancers
Northamptonshire Yeomanry
Royal Scots
Suffolk Regiment
East Yorkshire Regiment

Royal Scots Fusiliers
King's Own Scottish Borderers
Cameronians
Highland Light Infantry
Gordon Highlanders
Argyll and Sutherland Highlanders
Monmouthshire Regiment
Kensington Regiment
Herefordshire Light Infantry

and was also awarded to the:-

Royal Tank Regiment
Sherwood Rangers Yeomanry
3rd/4th County of London Yeomanry
Royal Northumberland Fusiliers
Somerset Light Infantry
Worcestershire Regiment
Duke of Wellington's Regiment
South Lancashire Regiment

King's Shropshire Light Infantry
Middlesex Regiment
Wiltshire Regiment
York and Lancaster Regiment
Seaforth Highlanders
Rifle Brigade
London Rifle Brigade
Black Watch

FONTENAY LE PESNIL

25th to 27th June, 1944

This was a hard-fought subsidiary Engagement involving 49th Division and 8th Armoured Brigade. The operation included the capture of Fontenay le Pesnil and Tessel Bretteville, and subsequent advance to Rauray.

The Honour was emblazoned by the:-

24th Lancers
Royal Lincolnshire Regiment
Duke of Wellington's Regiment

King's Own Yorkshire Light Infantry
York and Lancaster Regiment

and was also awarded to the:-

Sherwood Rangers Yeomanry
Royal Scots Fusiliers

Black Watch

CHEUX

26th to 27th June, 1944

In this subsidiary Action, VIII Corps fought hard to secure the general line le Haut du Bosq, Cheux, la Gaule, St. Mauvieu, before advancing to the River Odon. The following formations were involved: 15th Division, 31st Tank Brigade, 11th Armoured Division, 4th Armoured Brigade and 43rd Division.

The Honour was emblazoned by the:-

Fife and Forfar Yeomanry	Northamptonshire Yeomanry

and was also awarded to the:-

Royal Scots	Duke of Cornwall's Light Infantry
Royal Scots Fusiliers	Highland Light Infantry
King's Own Scottish Borderers	Seaforth Highlanders
Cameronians	

TOURMAUVILLE BRIDGE

27th June, 1944

In this subsidiary Engagement, 2/A, and S.H. closely followed by 23rd Hussars, having cleared Colleville, Mondrainville, and Tourville, seized intact the bridge north of Tourmauville and secured a bridgehead over the River Odon.

The Honour has been awarded to the:-

Argyll and Sutherland Highlanders

DEFENCE OF RAURAY

29th June to 2nd July, 1944

49th Division and 8th Armoured Brigade; 15th, 43rd and 53rd Divisions, 11th Armoured Division, 32nd Guard Brigade and 31st Tank Brigade, were involved in this subsidiary Action, which was a turning point in the campaign. Increasing enemy counter attacks, which forced the British on to the defensive, developed into a counter-offensive, which was crushingly defeated, a process in which the enemy lost some of his best troops, and was not again able to launch a force of equal size and quality.

The Honour was emblazoned by the:-

24th Lancers	Durham Light Infantry

and was also awarded to the:-

Sherwood Rangers Yeomanry	Royal Lincolnshire Regiment
3rd/4th County of London Yeomanry	Royal Scots Fusiliers
Northamptonshire Yeomanry	King's Own Scottish Borderers
Royal Scots	Black Watch
	Herefordshire Light Infantry

CAEN

4th to 18th July, 1944

I, VIII, XII and XXX Corps took part in this Battle, which cleared the city and surrounding industrial area of the enemy, and secured a footing on the Bourguebus Ridge.

The Honour was emblazoned by the:-

13th/18th Hussars	Devonshire Regiment
22nd Dragoons	Royal Welch Fusiliers
Staffordshire Yeomanry	South Wales Borderers
Royal Hampshire Regiment	King's Own Scottish Borderers
3rd/4th County of London Yeomanry	Inns of Court Regiment
South Staffordshire Regiment	Dorset Regiment
Northamptonshire Yeomanry	Middlesex Regiment
East Riding Yeomanry	Manchester Regiment
Royal Northumberland Fusiliers	North Staffordshire Regiment
Royal Warwickshire Regiment	Seaforth Highlanders
Lancashire Fusiliers	Royal Ulster Rifles

and was also awarded to the:-

Royal Scots Greys	Cameronians
Royal Tank Regiment	East Lancashire Regiment
Royal Scots	Black Watch
Royal Norfolk Regiment	Oxfordshire and Buckinghamshire Light Infantry
Royal Lincolnshire Regiment	King's Shropshire Light Infantry
Somerset Light Infantry	Wiltshire Regiment
East Yorkshire Regiment	York and Lancaster Regiment
	Argyll and Sutherland Highlanders

ORNE

8th to 9th July, 1944

In this subsidiary Action, in which 3rd Division, 59th Division, 3rd Canadian Division, and 27th, 33rd and 2nd Canadian Armoured Brigades took part, Caen north and west of the Rivers Orne and Vieil Odon was captured.

The Honour was awarded to the:-

Royal Lincolnshire Regiment	North Staffordshire Regiment
Middlesex Regiment	

HILL 112

10th to 11th July, 1944

This subsidiary Action was a valiant but unsuccessful fight by 43rd Division with 4th Armoured Brigade, 31st Tank Brigade, and 46th Brigade to secure Point 112 and Maltot.

The Honour was emblazoned by the:-

Royal Scots Greys	Duke of Cornwall's Light Infantry
Somerset Light Infantry	Wiltshire Regiment

and was also awarded to the:-

Royal Hampshire Regiment	Middlesex Regiment

ESQUAY

15th to 17th July, 1944

15th and 53rd Divisions were involved in this subsidiary Engagement. 15th Division had captured Esquay by the 16th July, and established their forward troops on a line westwards towards Bougy. 53rd Division continued the attack towards Evrecy, but were unsuccessful.

The Honour has been awarded to the:-

    Royal Scots   Manchester Regiment
    Royal Welch Fusiliers   Highland Light Infantry
    King's Own Scottish Borderers   Argyll and Sutherland Highlanders
    Oxfordshire and Buckinghamshire Light Infantry

NOYERS

15th to 18th July, 1944

This subsidiary Engagement was fought by 59th Division with 33rd Armoured Brigade. It failed to capture Noyers, but had the effect of retaining enemy formations west of the River Orne, while the thrust to the Bourguebus Ridge was being mounted.

The Honour is borne on the Colours of the:-

    South Staffordshire Regiment

and has also been awarded to the:-

    Northamptonshire Yeomanry   North Staffordshire Regiment

BOURGUEBUS RIDGE

18th to 23rd July, 1944

I, VIII and II Canadian Corps took part in this Battle, which covered the attack by VIII Corps (three armoured divisions) in Operation 'Goodwood', and the fighting by I Corps and II Canadian Corps on the flanks of the main thrust, as also the subsequent operations by the Canadians on the right in Operation 'Atlantic'.

The Honour was emblazoned by the:-

    23rd Hussars   South Lancashire Regiment
    Fife and Forfar Yeomanry   London Rifle Brigade
    Inns of Court Regiment   Monmouthshire Regiment
    Northamptonshire Yeomanry   Herefordshire Light Infantry
    East Riding Yeomanry

and was also awarded to the:-

    11th Hussars   Royal Lincolnshire Regiment
    13th/18th Hussars   East Yorkshire Regiment
    Royal Tank Regiment   Worcestershire Regiment
    3rd/4th County of London Yeomanry   King's Shropshire Light Infantry
    Honourable Artillery Company   Middlesex Regiment
    Welsh Guards   Wiltshire Regiment
    Royal Warwickshire Regiment   Rifle Brigade

CAGNY
18th to 19th July, 1944

This was an VIII Corps subsidiary section. Guards Armoured Division, 7th and 11th Armoured Divisions, and 51st Division (less 152nd Brigade) took part in this thrust east of the River Orne.

The Honour has been awarded to the:-

Inns of Court Regiment	Irish Guards
Grenadier Guards	Welsh Guards
Coldstream Guards	Royal Northumberland Fusiliers
Herefordshire Light Infantry	

TROARN
18th to 21st July, 1944

3rd Division and 152nd Brigade took part in this subsidiary Engagement, in which I Corps protected the flank of VIII Corps by capturing Touffreville, Sannerville, Bannerille, Cuillerville and woods to the north-east.

The Honour has been awarded to the:-

Staffordshire Yeomanry	South Lancashire Regiment
Royal Lincolnshire Regiment	King's Shropshire Light Infantry
East Yorkshire Regiment	Middlesex Regiment
King's Own Scottish Borderers	Seaforth Highlanders
Royal Ulster Rifles	

MALTOT
22nd to 23rd July, 1944

In this subsidiary Engagement, in which 43rd Division and 2nd Canadian Division took part, Maltot was taken.

The Honour was emblazoned by the:-

Wiltshire Regiment

and has also been awarded to the:-

Worcestershire Regiment

MONT PINCON
30th July – 9th August, 1944

VIII, XII and XXX Corps took part in this Battle. It covered the operations leading up to the capture of Mont Pincon, following the American break-out in the west.

The Honour was emblazoned by the:-

4th/7th Dragoon Guards	Welsh Guards
5th Dragoons Guards	Royal Warwickshire Regiment
13th/18th Hussars	Somerset Light Infantry
Northamptonshire Yeomanry	Gloucestershire Regiment
Grenadier Guards	Worcestershire Regiment
Coldstream Guards	Duke of Cornwall's Light Infantry

    Irish Guards   Middlesex Regiment
    Wiltshire Regiment   Queen's Westminsters

and has also been awarded to the:-

    Life Guards   Dorset Regiment
    Royal Horse Guards   King's Shropshire Light Infantry
    8th Hussars   King's Royal Rifle Corps
    11th Hussars   North Staffordshire Regiment
    Royal Tank Regiment   Highland Light Infantry
    Sherwood Rangers Yeomanry   Seaforth Highlanders
    Scots Guards   Argyll and Sutherland Highlanders
    Royal Scots   Rifle Brigade
    Queen's Royal Regiment   London Rifle Brigade
    East Yorkshire Regiment   Monmouthshire Regiment
    Royal Scots Fusiliers   Herefordshire Light Infantry
    Cheshire Regiment   King's Own Scottish Borderers
    Cameronians   Royal Hampshire Regiment

QUARRY HILL

30th July to 2nd August, 1944

In this subsidiary Engagement, 15th Division with 6th Guards Tank Brigade under command secured Quarry Hill (Point 309 to the west of the Bois du Homme) with 4/Tank Coldstream Guards, Glasgow Highlanders, and 7/Seaforth. The position was held firmly during ensuing days.

The Honour is borne on the Colours of the:-

    Scots Guards

and has also been awarded to the:-

    Coldstream Guards   Seaforth Highlanders
    Highland Light Infantry   Argyll and Sutherland Highlanders

JURQUES

30th July to 4th August, 1944

43rd Division, advancing to the Bois d'Homme in this subsidiary Engagement, ran into stubborn resistance near Brioquessard. Progress was made in face of stiff opposition about Cahagnes and St Pierre du Fresne, Jurques being captured on 2nd August.

The Honour has been awarded to the:-

    11th Hussars   Worcestershire Regiment
    Sherwood Rangers Yeomanry   Royal Hampshire Regiment

LA VARINIERE

4th to 9th August, 1944

In this subsidiary Engagement, 43rd Division and 8th Armoured Brigade advancing eastwards reached Lancers Variniere on 6th August. Here 5/Wiltshire found a strongly posted enemy. By that evening 13th/18th Hussars followed by 4/Wiltshires had reached the crest of Mont Pincon – Point 361. 5/D.C.L.I.

cleared Le Plessis Grimoult, and stiff fighting continued on 8th and 9th August, about Le Quesnee and Les Hameaux.

The Honour was awarded to the:-

    Worcestershire Regiment   Wiltshire Regiment

SOULEUVRE

30th July to 1st August, 1944

The operations by 11th Armoured and Guards Armoured Division in this subsidiary Engagement south of Caumont led to the capture of St Martin des Besaces, whilst the crossing of the River Souleuvre by 2/Household Cavalry Regiment and 2/Northamptonshire Yeomanry led to the capture of Le Beny Bocage.

The Honour is borne on the Standards and Colours of the:

    Life Guards   Herefordshire Light Infantry
    Royal Horse Guards

and was also awarded to the:-

    King's Shropshire Light Infantry   Monmouthshire Regiment

CATHEOLLES

2nd to 5th August, 1944

This subsidiary Engagement covered fighting by Guards Armoured Division and 15th Division against stubborn resistance.

The Honour is borne on the Colours of the:-

    Inns of Court Regiment

LE PERIER RIDGE

2nd to 8th August, 1944

In this subsidiary Engagement 11th Armoured Division, advancing beyond the Souleuvre, was halted on the Vire-Vassy road and withdrew to Le Perier Ridge. Here, with 3rd Division, they defeated enemy counter-attacks with tanks and infantry.

The Honour was emblazoned by the:-

    23rd Hussars   Monmouthshire Regiment
    Fife and Forfar Yeomanry

and was also awarded to the:-

    Royal Norfolk Regiment   Rifle Brigade
    King's Shropshire Light Infantry   London Rifle Brigade

BRIEUX BRIDGEHEAD

6th to 8th August, 1944

59th Division, in this subsidiary Engagement, withstood for two days heavy and concerted counter-attacks with tanks and infantry. 53rd Division was also involved.

The Honour was emblazoned by the:-

    Royal Norfolk Regiment   North Staffordshire Regiment

ST PIERRE LA VIEILLE

9th to 16th August, 1944

50th Division and 43rd Division were concerned in this Engagement. Strong enemy rearguards fought stubbornly about St Pierre.

The Honour has been awarded to the:-

- 5th Dragoons Guards
- 13th/18th Hussars
- Devonshire Regiment
- East Yorkshire Regiment
- Green Howards
- Cheshire Regiment
- Royal Hampshire Regiment
- Dorset Regiment
- Durham Light Infantry

ESTRY

6th to 12th August, 1944

15th Division, with 6th Guards Tank Brigade, launched attacks, in this Engagement, towards Lassy, Point 208, and Estry, which met with stubborn resistance. Fighting for Estry was fierce, and elsewhere no progress was made.

The Honour has been awarded to the:-

- Coldstream Guards
- Scots Guards
- Royal Scots Fusiliers
- King's Own Scottish Borderers
- Cameronians
- Highland Light Infantry
- Argyll and Sutherland Highlanders

NOIREAU CROSSING

14th to 17th August, 1944

This Engagement, involving 43rd Division, covered the river crossing on the 15th between, roughly, Berjou and the mill at Cahan, and the further progress on the 16th and 17th in face of considerable resistance and counter-attacks.

The Honour was awarded to the:-

- Life Guards
- Royal Horse Guards
- Sherwood Rangers Yeomanry
- Somerset Light Infantry
- Worcestershire Regiment
- Duke of Cornwall's Light Infantry

FALAISE

7th to 22nd August, 1944

This Battle was fought by First Canadian Army, with I Corps under command, and Second Army, with XII and XXX Corps. The object was to capture Falaise and to close the gap between it and Argentan, thereby trapping the German forces between the Canadian, British, American and French forces.

The Honour was emblazoned by the:-

Royal Scots Greys
22nd Dragoons
Lothians and Border Horse
Northamptonshire Yeomanry
Suffolk Regiment
Royal Scots Fusiliers

Gloucestershire Regiment
East Lancashire Regiment
South Staffordshire Regiment
South Lancashire Regiment
Welch Regiment
Monmouthshire Regiment
Herefordshire Light Infantry

and has also been awarded to the:-

Royal Tank Regiment
3rd/4th County of London Yeomanry
Royal Northumberland Fusiliers
Royal Warwickshire Regiment
Royal Welch Fusiliers
South Wales Borderers
Black Watch
King's Shropshire Light Infantry

Middlesex Regiment
King's Royal Rifle Corps
Manchester Regiment
Highland Light Infantry
Seaforth Highlanders
Cameron Highlanders
Argyll and Sutherland Highlanders
Rifle Brigade
London Rifle Brigade

FALAISE ROAD

7th to 9th August, 1944

In this subsidiary Action, 3rd Canadian Division, 1st Polish Armoured Division, and 51st Division advanced astride the Falaise Road from Verriere-Bourguebus to the River Laison.

The Honour is borne on the Colours of the:-

Black Watch

and was also awarded to the:-

Lothians and Border Horse
Northamptonshire Yeomanry

Seaforth Highlanders
Cameron Highlanders

LAISON

14th to 17th August, 1944

This subsidiary Action covered the advance over the Laison by II Canadian Corps and their subsequent capture of Falaise in conjunction with the advance from Bonnoeil of 53rd Division (XII Corps).

The Honour has been awarded to the:-

Lothians and Border Horse.

DIVES CROSSING

17th to 20th August, 1944

This Engagement involved the river crossing, in face of opposition, by 6th Airborne Division west of Dozule, and by 49th Division about Mezidon, and included 51st Division's operations at Ecajeul and St Maclou. This Honour is borne on the Guidon of the Derbyshire Yeomanry.

and has been awarded to the:-

8th Hussars

Seaforth Highlanders

11th Hussars
Northamptonshire Yeomanry

Argyll and Sutherland Highlanders
Parachute Regiment
Commando Association

LA VIE CROSSING

18th to 20th August, 1944

This Engagement was an opposed river crossing, by 49th Division west of St Pair du Mont, and by 51st Division at Grandchamp and St Julien le Faucon. The latter was a gallant operation.

The Honour has been awarded to the:-

11th Hussars
Derbyshire Yeomanry
East Riding Yeomanry
Royal Scots Fusiliers
Black Watch

York and Lancaster Regiment
Seaforth Highlanders
Gordon Highlanders
Cameron Highlanders

LISIEUX

21st to 23rd August, 1944

In this Engagement, 51st Division and 7th Armoured Division cleared Lisieux.

The Honour was emblazoned by the:-

East Riding Yeomanry

and was also awarded to the:-

5th Dragoon Guards
11th Hussars
Derbyshire Yeomanry

Northamptonshire Yeomanry
Seaforth Highlanders

LA TOUQUES CROSSING

22nd to 23rd August, 1944

In this Engagement, operations took place by 49th Division across the River la Touques about Ouilly le Vicomte, and by 6th Airborne Division at Pont L'Eveque. The latter was a particularly stubborn operation.

The Honour has been awarded to the:-

11th Hussars
Royal Scots Fusiliers

Parachute Regiment
York and Lancaster Regiment

RISLE CROSSING

25th to 27th August, 1944

This Engagement involved the crossing on a broad front between Pont Authou and Pont Audemer, and subsequent operations, by 7th Armoured Division and 49th Division.

The Honour has been awarded to the:-

5th Dragoons Guards
11th Hussars

Gloucestershire Regiment
South Wales Borderers

FORET DE BRETONNE

28th to 30th August, 1944

49th and 51st Divisions were involved in this Engagement, which comprised operations to clear the wooded meanders of the River Seine east of the Risle.

The Honour was awarded to the:-

    East Riding Yeomanry   York and Lancaster Regiment

SEINE, 1944

25th to 28th August

In this Action, 43rd Division assaulted across the Seine at Vernon on the 25th August against stiff opposition and formed a bridgehead. On the 27th August, 4th Canadian Armoured Division, 3rd Canadian Division, and 15th Division assaulted across the river at Criquebeuf, Elbeuf, and near Louviers respectively. Opposition varied but built up against the bridgeheads formed.

The Honour was emblazoned by the:-

    15th/19th Hussars   Wiltshire Regiment
    Worcestershire Regiment

and was also awarded to the:-

    4th/7th Dragoons Guards   Middlesex Regiment
    Sherwood Rangers Yeomanry   Highland Light Infantry
    Somerset Light Infantry

AMIENS, 1944

31st August

By a successful night advance, 11th Armoured Division surprised the enemy in this Engagement, and by capturing the town frustrated the German plans for defence of the line of the Somme.

The Honour was emblazoned by the:-

    23rd Hussars   Inns of Court Regiment

and was also awarded to the:-

    Life Guards   Royal Horse Guards

BRUSSELS

3rd September, 1944

In this Engagement, Guards Armoured Division set off from Douai early on 3rd September, overcome resistance at Pont A Marq, Leuse and Hal, and liberated Brussels that evening – a sharp thrust of 70 miles.

The Honour is borne on the Standards and Colours of the:-

    Life Guards   Welsh Guards
    Royal Horse Guards

ANTWERP

4th to 7th September, 1944

11th Armoured Division met with stiff opposition in the city in this Engagement. During the night 5th/6th September, 4/K.S.L.I. assaulted across the Albert Canal, but was pinned there by enemy infantry and tanks until withdrawn on 7th September.

The Honour was emblazoned by the:-

    23rd Hussars   London Rifle Brigade
    Inns of Court Regiment   Monmouthshire Regiment
    King's Shropshire Light Infantry   Herefordshire Light Infantry

and was also awarded to the:-

    Honourable Artillery Company   Rifle Brigade

HECHTEL

7th to 12th September, 1944

This Engagement covered the bitter defence of the village, against the Welsh Guards Group of Guards Armoured Division, by German S.S. and Parachute troops, 500 of whom were taken prisoner, and also sharp fighting nearby at Helchteren.

The Honour is borne on the Colours and Appointments of the:-

    Welsh Guards   London Rifle Brigade
    Herefordshire Light Infantry

and has also been awarded to the:-

    15th/19th Hussars   Rifle Brigade
    Inns of Court Regiment

GHEEL

8th – 12th May, 1944

In this Engagement, 50th Division established a bridgehead across the Albert Canal, and extended it to include Gheel.

The Honour is borne on the Guidon and Colours of the:-

    Sherwood Rangers Yeomanry   Durham Light Infantry

and was also awarded to the:-

    East Yorkshire Regiment   Cheshire Regiment
    Green Howards

HEPPEN

8th to 9th September, 1944

In this Engagement, the Coldstream Guards Group of Guards Armoured Division fought all day to reach Heppen, finally capturing it on the 9th, and breaking up a German counter-attack.

The Honour has been awarded to the:-

    Coldstream Guards

NEERPELT

10th September, 1944

Better known regimentally as 'Joe's Bridge', this Engagement was the scene of the seizure, principally by the Irish Guards, of a bridge over the Meuse-Escaut Canal.

The Honour is borne on the colours of the Irish Guards and was awarded to the:-

    Life Guards   Royal Horse Guards

AART

14th to 20th September, 1944

In this Engagement, 15th Division established a bridgehead over the Meuse-Escaut Canal north of Gheel, and some hard fighting took place before the bridgehead was finally withdrawn.

The Honour is borne on the Colours of the:-

    Royal Scots

and was also awarded to the:-

Royal Scots Fusiliers	Argyll and Sutherland Highlanders
King's Own Scottish Borderers	Highland Light Infantry

NEDERRIJN

17th to 27th September, 1944

This Battle, in which VIII, XII, XXX and I Airborne Corps took part, was fought to obtain a springboard beyond the Rhine from which to attack the Ruhr. A carpet of airborne troops was laid across the waterways on the axis chosen, up which ground forces advanced at speed, while further ground forces widened the corridor. Opposition was stronger than was expected, and weather was worse; these imposed delays. A bridgehead was gained over the Waal, but the north bank of the Nederrijn could not be held.

The Honour was emblazoned by the:-

Life Guards	1st Royal Dragoons
Royal Horse Guards	15th/19th Hussars
4th/7th Dragoons Guards	Duke of Cornwall's Light Infantry

and has also been awarded to the:-

8th Hussars	Worcestershire Regiment
Royal Tank Regiment	East Lancashire Regiment
Sherwood Rangers Yeomanry	Royal Hampshire Regiment
Coldstream Guards	King's Shropshire Light Infantry
Welsh Guards	Middlesex Regiment
Royal Scots	Manchester Regiment
Royal Northumberland Fusiliers	Highland Light Infantry
Devonshire Regiment	Seaforth Highlanders
Somerset Light Infantry	Rifle Brigade
East Yorkshire Regiment	London Rifle Brigade
Green Howards	Monmouthshire Regiment
Royal Scots Fusiliers	Cheshire Regiment
Royal Welch Fusiliers	King's Own Scottish Borderers

Cameronians
Wiltshire Regiment

Royal Lincolnshire Regiment

ARNHEM, 1944

17th to 26th September

In this subsidiary Action, in which 1st Airborne Division and part of 1st Polish Independent Parachute Group took part, the Division fought hard from 17th to 19th September, to capture Arnhem; thereafter, until the 25th, they hung on grimly awaiting relief. On the 24th, 4/Dorset assaulted across the river to cover the withdrawal.

The Honour was emblazoned by the:-

King's Own Scottish Borderers
Border Regiment
South Staffordshire Regiment
Parachute Regiment
Glider Pilot Regiment
Dorset Regiment

NIJMEGEN

19th to 20th September, 1944

Guards Armoured Division fought this subsidiary Engagement, with 82nd U.S. Airborne Division. The German defence of the town was very stubborn. Finally, the Americans made a very gallant daylight assault crossing just west of the town, and the Grenadier Guards successfully rushed the bridge.

The Honour is borne on the Colours of the:-

Grenadier Guards
Irish Guards

and was also awarded to the:-

Life Guards
Royal Horse Guards

VEGHEL

22nd to 23rd September, 1944

In this subsidiary Engagement, the XXX Corps axis was attacked at Veghel after two divisions had passed through to the Nijmegen area. The axis was cleared by 32nd Guards Brigade from the north, and 101st U.S. Airborne Division and 44/R.T.R. from the south.

The Honour has been awarded to the:-

1st Royal Dragoons

BEST

22nd to 27th September, 1944

In this subsidiary Engagement, repeated attacks were made by 15th Division on the strong enemy positions here, but not till 27th September could they be dislodged.

The Honour has been awarded to the:-

8th Hussars
Royal Scots
Royal Scots Fusiliers
King's Own Scottish Borderers
Cameronians
Highland Light Infantry
Seaforth Highlanders

LE HAVRE

10th to 12th September, 1944

In this Engagement, 49th and 51st Division captured the port by assault with special armour through well organised ground defences.

The Honour was emblazoned by the:-

22nd Dragoons   Northamptonshire Yeomanry
South Wales Borderers

and was also awarded to the:-

Lothians and Border Horse   King's Own Yorkshire Light Infantry
Honourable Artillery Company   York and Lancaster Regiment
Royal Lincolnshire Regiment   Seaforth Highlanders
Royal Scots Fusiliers   Cameron Highlanders
Gloucestershire Regiment   Black Watch
Essex Regiment   Middlesex Regiment

BOULOGNE, 1944

17th to 22nd September

In this Engagement, 3rd Canadian Division captured the citadel on the 18th September, but some of the outer forts and defences held out until the 22nd.

The Honour was emblazoned by the:-

Lothians and Border Horse.

CALAIS, 1944

25th September to 1st October.

In this Engagement, 3rd Canadian Division captured the port and Cap Griz Nez.

The Honour was awarded to the:-

Lothians and Border Horse.

ANTWERP-TURNHOUT CANAL

24th to 29th September, 1944

This was a I Corps Engagement. 2nd Canadian Division assaulted across the canal at Lochtenberg, but was unable to establish a bridgehead. 49th Division assaulted across at Ryckevorsel, and expanded this bridgehead against considerable resistance.

The Honour was emblazoned by the:-

Royal Lincolnshire Regiment   Kensington Regiment
York and Lancaster Regiment

and was also awarded to the:-

Royal Leicestershire Regiment   King's Own Yorkshire Light Infantry
Royal Scots Fusiliers   South Wales Borderers
Essex Regiment

SCHELDT

1st October to 8th November, 1944

In this Battle, the Germans were holding firmly on both sides of the Scheldt estuary to deny us the use of Antwerp. Walcheren Island was flooded by air Action, and a two-pronged attack cleared South Beveland to the north and the Breskens Pocket to the south. Walcheren Island was then assaulted and German control of the Scheldt eliminated.

First Canadian Army, with 52nd Division and 4th Special Service Brigade under command, and I Corps (49th Division, 34th Tank Brigade, 4th Canadian Armoured Division) were involved.

The Honour was emblazoned by the:-

Fife and Forfar Yeomanry	Manchester Regiment
Royal Leicestershire Regiment	Highland Light Infantry
Royal Scots Fusiliers	Cameronians

and was also awarded to the:-

Royal Tank Regiment	Essex Regiment
Lothians and Border Horse	York and Lancaster Regiment
Royal Scots	South Wales Borderers
King's Own Scottish Borderers	

SOUTH BEVELAND

24th to 31st October, 1944

52nd Division (less 155th Brigade) took part in this subsidiary Engagement. After an advance by 2nd Canadian Division over appalling going, 52nd Division crossed the Scheldt in amphibious vehicles, and the two divisions pressed westwards.

The Honour has been awarded to the:-

Royal Scots Fusiliers	Highland Light Infantry
Cameronians	

WALCHEREN CAUSEWAY

31st October to 4th November, 1944

In this subsidiary Engagement, 5th Canadian Brigade and 157th Brigade met very severe opposition. On the night of 2nd November, 6/Cameronians crossed the Slooe Channel to the south, followed later by 5/H.L.I., who linked up with 1/Glasgow Highlanders in the Canadian bridgehead on 4th November.

The Honour was emblazoned by the:-

Highland Light Infantry

and was also awarded to the:-

Cameronians	Manchester Regiment

FLUSHING

1st to 4th November, 1944

In this subsidiary Engagement, No. 4 Commando led the assault from Breskens followed up by 155th Brigade. German resistance was cleared area by area, but only ceased after a dawn assault on 3rd November, on their headquarters in the Hotel Britannia.

The Honour is borne on the Colours of the:-

    Royal Scots   King's Own Scottish Borderers

and was also awarded to the:-

    Manchester Regiment   Commando Association

WESTKAPELLE

1st to 3rd November, 1944

In this subsidiary Engagement, 4th Special Service Brigade landed under heavy fire from coast defences, and reduced the shore batteries in succession.

The Honour was emblazoned by the:-

    Lothians and Border Horse

and was also awarded to the:-

    Commando Association

LOWER MAAS

20th October to 7th November, 1944

In this Action, XII Corps (7th Armoured Division, 15th, 51st and 53rd Divisions) and I Corps (1st Polish Armoured Division, 104th U.S. Division, 49th Division, and 4th Canadian Armoured Division) advanced respectively from the east and south of the Lower Maas. The Germans fought stubbornly to oppose this advance at Schijndel, s'Hertogenbosch, Loon op Zand, River Mark, Welberg, Moerdijk, and at many other points.

The Honour was emblazoned by the:-

5th Dragoons Guards	East Riding Yeomanry
8th Hussars	Royal Welch Fusiliers
22nd Dragoons	East Lancashire Regiment
Derbyshire Yeomanry	Welch Regiment
Northamptonshire Yeomanry	Manchester Regiment
Monmouthshire Regiment	

and was also awarded to the:-

3rd/4th County of London Yeomanry	York and Lancaster Regiment
Queen's Royal Regiment	Highland Light Infantry
Royal Scots Fusiliers	Seaforth Highlanders
Black Watch	Gordon Highlanders
Oxfordshire and Buckinghamshire Light Infantry	Cameron Highlanders
King's Own Yorkshire Light Infantry	Argyll and Sutherland Highlanders
Middlesex Regiment	Rifle Brigade

AAM
1st to 4th October, 1944

43rd Division, with 5th Guards Armoured Brigade, 69th Brigade and 6/H.L.I. knew this Engagement better as the fighting on 'the Island'. The Germans made a very determined effort to break through the Nijmegen bridgehead on 1st and 2nd October. Some positions at Aam were overrun, but the attacks were held and the position restored by counter-attacks.

The Honour was emblazoned by the:-
    Dorset Regiment

and was also awarded to the:-
    Irish Guards   Cheshire Regiment
    East Yorkshire Regiment

OPHEUSDEN
5th – 7th October, 1944

101st U.S. Airborne Division relieved 43rd Division, and attacked Opheusden, in this Engagement, with great success, but a German counter-attack next day led to such fierce fighting that 5/D.C.L.I. was ordered to counter attack. After hard fighting they and the Americans threw the enemy back.

The Honour has been awarded to the:-
    Duke of Cornwall's Light Infantry

VENRAIJ
12th to 18th October, 1944

This was an VIII Corps Action, in which 3rd Division, 6th Guards Tank Brigade and 11th Armoured Division took part. The operations were the preliminaries to the clearance of the west bank of the River Maas.

The Honour was emblazoned by the:-
    23rd Hussars   Suffolk Regiment
    Westminster Dragoons   King's Shropshire Light Infantry
    Royal Warwickshire Regiment Herefordshire Light Infantry
    Royal Norfolk Regiment

and was also awarded to the:-
    15th/19th Hussars   King's Own Scottish Borderers
    Coldstream Guards   South Lancashire Regiment
    Royal Lincolnshire Regiment   Middlesex Regiment
    East Yorkshire Regiment

ASTEN and MEIJEL
27th October to 5th November, 1944

15th Division and 7th U.S. Armoured Division, under VIII Corps, fought this Engagement in which a series of German armoured attacks forced back the Americans, who were holding a wide front. 15th Division were brought back from Tilburg and took over the American left sector. They attacked next day, and so did the Germans who, however, withdrew slowly after two days of hard fighting.

'Asten' has been awarded to the:-

  Cameronians   Highland Light Infantry

'Meijel' is borne on the Guidon of the:-   Westminster Dragoons

and has also been awarded to the:-

  Coldstream Guards   Middlesex Regiment
  Royal Scots   Seaforth Highlanders
  Royal Scots Fusiliers   Argyll and Sutherland Highlanders
  King's Own Scottish Borderers

GEILENKIRCHEN

18th to 23rd November, 1944

In this Action, 84th US Division, 43rd Division and 8th Armoured Brigade attacked past the town on either flank. The Americans then cleared it. Rain now made the ground impassable to tanks, but the infantry continued to advance against increasing enemy resistance. This finally turned into fierce counter-attacks which forced them on to the defensive.

The Honour was emblazoned by the:-

  4th/7th Dragoon Guards   Sherwood Rangers Yeomanry
  13th/18th Hussars   Worcestershire Regiment
  Duke of Cornwall's Light Infantry   Dorset Regiment

and has also been awarded to the:

  Lothians and Border Horse   Middlesex Regiment
  Somerset Light Infantry

VENLO POCKET

14th November to 3rd December, 1944

In this Action, XII Corps (51st Division, 53rd Division, 7th Armoured Division, 49th Division) and VIII Corps (15th Division, 11th Armoured Division, 3rd Division) took part. The enemy was cleared out of his last holding west of the Maas, till finally only Blerick was left, when 44th Brigade, in a well organised and heavily supported attack, rapidly reduced the town.

The Honour was emblazoned by the:-

  22nd Dragoons   Westminster Dragoons
  23rd Hussars   East Riding Yeomanry

and has also been awarded to the:-

  Royal Scots Greys   Manchester Regiment
  Royal Tank Regiment   Seaforth Highlanders
  Northamptonshire Yeomanry   Gordon Highlanders
  Scots Guards   Cameron Highlanders
  Royal Scots   Royal Ulster Rifles
  Royal Lincolnshire Regiment   Argyll and Sutherland Highlanders
  Royal Scots Fusiliers   Monmouthshire Regiment
  Royal Welch Fusiliers   Herefordshire Light Infantry
  King's Own Scottish Borderers   Kensington Regiment
  Black Watch   Middlesex Regiment

ROER

16th to 31st January, 1945

This was a XII Corps Engagement, involving 7th Armoured Division, 43rd Division, 52nd Division, 6th Guards Tank Brigade, and 1st Commando Brigade. The clearance of this area brought 21st Army Group to the Roer-Maas line, with only the Rhineland between them and the Rhine. In places the Germans fought fiercely, but some of their forces here were not of high quality.

The Honour was emblazoned by the:-

- 5th Dragoons Guards
- 8th Hussars
- 11th Hussars
- 13th/18th Hussars
- Westminster Dragoons
- Manchester Regiment
- Queen's Westminsters

and was also awarded to the:-

- 4th/7th Dragoons Guards
- Sherwood Rangers Yeomanry
- Lothians and Border Horse
- Coldstream Guards
- Royal Scots
- Queen's Royal Regiment
- Devonshire Regiment
- Somerset Light Infantry
- King's Own Scottish Borderers
- Cameronians
- Royal Hampshire Regiment
- King's Royal Rifle Corps
- Wiltshire Regiment
- Durham Light Infantry
- Highland Light Infantry
- Royal Scots Fusiliers
- Rifle Brigade

ZETTEN

18th to 21st January, 1945

In this Engagement, fought by 49th Division, a strong German attack broke into the very extended positions held by the Division. The front was stabilised and the ground regained with 400 prisoners taken.

The Honour was emblazoned by the:-

- Essex Regiment

and has also been awarded to the:-

- Royal Leicestershire Regiment
- South Wales Borderers
- Gloucestershire Regiment
- Kensington Regiment

OURTHE

3rd to 14th January, 1945

In this Action, when the American Armies counter-attacked to regain the Ardennes, XXX Corps (6th Airborne Division, 51st Division, 53rd Division, 29th and 33rd Armoured Brigades) advanced to clear the area in the fork made by the two branches of the River Ourthe. Heavy fighting took place at Bure and Grimbiemont, and on a smaller scale at many other points.

The Honour was emblazoned by the:-

- 23rd Hussars
- Fife and Forfar Yeomanry
- Northamptonshire Yeomanry
- East Lancashire Regiment
- Monmouthshire Regiment

and was also awarded to the:-

Derbyshire Yeomanry
East Riding Yeomanry
Royal Welch Fusiliers
Black Watch
Oxfordshire and Buckinghamshire Light Infantry

Manchester Regiment
Highland Light Infantry
Seaforth Highlanders
Argyll and Sutherland Highlanders
Parachute Regiment

RHINELAND

8th February to 10th March, 1945

Between the Maas and the Rhine lay the last German stronghold barring 21st Army Group from the Ruhr. A concerted attack from north and south was prevented by the Germans flooding the Roer valley. So First Canadian Army, attacking from the north, had all the enemy reinforcements thrown in against it. Then, as the flood subsided, Ninth U.S. Army made a fast advance from the south. The two armies linked up, the last pocked of Germans was eliminated, and only the Rhine separated the Allied Armies from the Ruhr.

In this Battle, XXX Corps and II Canadian Corps fought under First Canadian Army, and the following formations were involved: 51st Division, 53rd Division, 15th Division, 2nd Canadian Division, 3rd Canadian Division, 43rd Division, Guards Armoured Division, 52nd Division, 4th Canadian Armoured Division, 11th Armoured Division, 3rd Division, 1st Commando Brigade, Independent Armoured Brigades, and regiments of 79th Armoured Division.

The Honour has been emblazoned by the:-

4th/7th Dragoons Guards
13th/18th Hussars
15th/19th Hussars
Derbyshire Yeomanry
Fife and Forfar Yeomanry
Coldstream Guards
Scots Guards
Irish Guards
Royal Northumberland Fusiliers

Royal Norfolk Regiment
Royal Lincolnshire Regiment
Somerset Light Infantry
Cameronians
Duke of Cornwall's Light Infantry
South Lancashire Regiment
King's Royal Rifle Corps
Seaforth Highlanders
Queen's Westminsters
Monmouthshire Regiment

and has also been awarded to the:-

Royal Tank Regiment
Sherwood Rangers Yeomanry
3rd/4th County of London Yeomanry
Welsh Guards
Royal Scots
Royal Warwickshire Regiment
East Yorkshire Regiment
Royal Scots Fusiliers
Royal Welch Fusiliers
King's Own Scottish Borderers
Worcestershire Regiment
East Lancashire Regiment

Royal Hampshire Regiment
Black Watch
Oxfordshire and Buckinghamshire Light Infantry
King's Shropshire Light Infantry
Middlesex Regiment
Wiltshire Regiment
Manchester Regiment
Highland Light Infantry
Gordon Highlanders
Cameron Highlanders
Argyll & Sutherland Highlanders
Herefordshire Light Infantry

REICHSWALD

8th to 13th February, 1945

In this subsidiary Action, XXX Corps broke into the Reichswald on a four-divisional front (51st Division, 15th Division, and 2nd Canadian Division). They rolled up the first felt of enemy defences, drove the Germans out of the forest, and secured the low ground east of the Maas up to and including the Gennep-Hekkens road.

The Honour was emblazoned by the:-

22nd Dragoons	Manchester Regiment
Royal Welch Fusiliers	Highland Light Infantry
East Lancashire Regiment	Gordon Highlanders
Welch Regiment	Cameron Highlanders
Oxfordshire and Buckinghamshire Light Infantry	

and was also awarded to the:-

Derbyshire Yeomanry	Cameronians
Lothians and Border Horse	Black Watch
Grenadier Guards	Middlesex Regiment
Coldstream Guards	Seaforth Highlanders
Scots Guards	Argyll and Sutherland Highlanders
Royal Scots	Monmouthshire Regiment
Royal Scots Fusiliers	King's Own Scottish Borderers

WAAL FLATS

8th to 15th February, 1945

In this subsidiary Engagement, 3rd Canadian Division attacked across the flooded ground south of the Waal in amphibious vehicles. Strongly defended localities were met and overpowered in stiff fighting.

The Honour has been awarded to the:-

13th/18th Hussars

CLEVE

9th to 11th February, 1945

In this subsidiary Engagement, 15th Division seized the Materborn feature but could not capture Cleve. 129th Brigade (43rd Division), advancing by night through Cleve towards Goch, met enemy armoured reinforcements arriving. Fierce fighting developed into which 214th Brigade (43rd Division) entered. Meanwhile, 15th Division pressed forward on the left, and the Germans were driven back.

The Honour was emblazoned by the:-

4th/7th Dragoons Guards	Wiltshire Regiment

and was also awarded to the:-

Sherwood Rangers Yeomanry	King's Own Scottish Borderers
Coldstream Guards	King's Royal Rifle Corps
Scots Guards	Gordon Highlanders
Royal Scots	Queen's Westminster
Somerset Light Infantry	Royal Scots Fusiliers

MOYLAND and MOYLAND WOOD

14th to 21st February, 1945

In this subsidiary Engagement, 46th Brigade and 10/H.L.I. fought their way forward, against very stiff resistance, from Cleve almost to Moyland, and captured the high ground to the east by 16th February. 3rd Canadian Division with S/Tank S.G. attacked on their right, and opened the main road through Moyland.

The honour of 'Moyland' has been awarded to the:-

    Coldstream Guards   Cameronians
    Scots Guards   Seaforth Highlanders

'Moyland Wood' has been awarded to the:-

    Highland Light Infantry

WEEZE

24th February to 2nd March, 1945

In this subsidiary Engagement, 53rd Division advanced from Goch, clearing Host and Rottum in tow days' fighting, but was held up by the enemy just short of Weeze. An enemy counter-attack delayed the next phase. After a two brigade attack on the town, in which stiff opposition was met, the Germans withdrew.

The Honour was emblazoned by the:-

    Royal Welch Fusiliers   East Lancashire Regiment

and was also awarded to the:-

    Sherwood Rangers Yeomanry   Highland Light Infantry
    Manchester Regiment   Monmouthshire Regiment

HOCHWALD

26th February to 4th March, 1945

This was a II Canadian Corps subsidiary Action, in which 11th Armoured Division, 214th Brigade (43rd Division), 3rd Division and Guards Armoured Division played a part. 4th Canadian Armoured Division made the main thrust into the Hochwald defences. After fierce fighting the Canadians were unable to exploit, but the other thrusts in the forests north and south of the railway slowly drove the enemy back.

The Honour is borne on the Guidons and Colours of the:-

    Royal Scots Greys   King's Shropshire Light Infantry
    15th/19th Hussars   Herefordshire Light Infantry

and was also awarded to the:-

    3rd/4th County of London Yeomanry   Somerset Light Infantry
    Coldstream Guards   South Lancashire Regiment
    Scots Guards   King's Royal Rifle Corps
    Irish Guards   Monmouthshire Regiment
    Royal Norfolk Regiment
    Royal Lincolnshire Regiment

SCHADDENHOF
27th to 28th February, 1945

In this subsidiary Engagement, the bridge over the Muhlen Fleuth by which Weeze could be outflanked was captured intact by one company of 2/E. Yorks (3rd Division). Here they were strongly counter-attacked; ammunition ran short, but supplies got through and another company reinforced them, enabling them to hold their ground though suffering heavy casualties.

The Honour was emblazoned by the:-

    East Yorkshire Regiment

XANTEN
8th to 9th March, 1945

In this subsidiary Engagement, 2nd Canadian Division and 43rd Division met stiff opposition in their attack on Xanten.

The Honour has been awarded to the:-

Somerset Light Infantry	Wiltshire Regiment

RHINE
23rd March to 1st April, 1945

In this Battle, 21st Army Group employed Second Army, First Canadian Army, and Ninth U.S. Army. The Battle covered the assault crossing by 15th and 51st Divisions, and 1st Commando Brigade, during 23rd/24th March, followed by 6th Airborne Division on the 24th; the subsequent enlargement of the bridgehead, including the capture of crossings over the River Ijssel, preparatory to the break-out; the latter including the operations by 15th, 51st, 52nd and 6th Airborne Divisions, together with 1st Commando Brigade; and also the advances by 7th Armoured Division to Borken, 53rd Division to Bocholt, 3rd Division to beyond Werth, 53rd Division beyond Anholt to Varsseveld and Silvolde, and by 3rd Canadian Division to Emmerich and Hoch Elten.

The Honour was emblazoned by the:-

4th/7th Dragoons Guards	Somerset Light Infantry
1st Royal Dragoons	Royal Scots Fusiliers
8th Hussars	Royal Welch Fusiliers
11th Hussars	King's Own Scottish Borderers
15th/19th Hussars	Cameronians
22nd Dragoons	Royal Hampshire Regiment
Royal Tank Regiment	Black Watch
Sherwood Rangers Yeomanry	Oxfordshire and Buckinghamshire Light Infantry
Staffordshire Yeomanry	Royal Berkshire Regiment
Fife and Forfar Yeomanry	Middlesex Regiment
3rd/4th County of London Yeomanry	Highland Light Infantry
Inns of Court Regiment	Gordon Highlanders
Northamptonshire Yeomanry	Cameron Highlanders
East Riding Yeomanry	Royal Ulster Rifles
Honourable Artillery Company	Argyll and Sutherland Highlanders
Grenadier Guards	Glider Pilot Regiment

Royal Scots	Parachute Regiment
Devonshire Regiment	Queen's Westminsters

and was also awarded to the:-

13th/18th Hussars	Dorset Regiment
Coldstream Guards	King's Royal Rifle Corps
Scots Guards	Wiltshire Regiment
Irish Guards	Manchester Regiment
Worcestershire Regiment	Seaforth Highlanders
East Lancashire Regiment	Monmouthshire Regiment
Duke of Cornwall's Light Infantry	Commando Association

IBBENBUREN

1st to 6th April, 1945

In this Engagement, 159th Brigade (11th Armoured Division) gained the crest of the Teutoburger Wald ridge, but were driven off by a strong force of German officer cadets and N.C.Os. 131st Brigade (7th Armoured Division) arrived to meet the German counter-attack in flank, regained the ridge and nearly reached Ibbenburen. 155th Brigade (52nd Division) attacked an secured the ridge west of the town, and 71st Brigade (53rd Division) passed through and crushed the final resistance.

The Honour is borne on the Guidon and Colours of the:-

15/19th Hussars	Monmouthshire Regiment

and was also awarded to the:-

5th Dragoons Guards	Oxfordshire and Buckinghamshire Light Infantry
11th Hussars	King's Shropshire Light Infantry
Devonshire Regiment	Manchester Regiment
Royal Welch Fusiliers	Durham Light Infantry
King's Own Scottish Borderers	Highland Light Infantry
East Lancashire Regiment	Herefordshire Light Infantry

LINGEN

2nd to 5th April, 1945

Guards Armoured Division and 3rd Division (less 8th Bde.), were involved in this Engagement, which began with the wild night drive of the Scots-Welsh Guards Group. They just failed to seize a bridge over the Ems in Lingen. The fighting continued with the Coldstream Group's capture intact of the bridge at Altenlingen, where Capt. Ian Liddell won the V.C. Then 3rd Division crossed here, assaulted over the Dortmund-Ems Canal, took the town's defences from the rear, and cleared it in hard fighting.

The Honour was awarded to the:-

Life Guards	Royal Warwickshire Regiment
Royal Horse Guards	Royal Norfolk Regiment
Staffordshire Yeomanry	Royal Lincolnshire Regiment
Coldstream Guards	King's Own Scottish Borderers
Scots Guards	King's Shropshire Light Infantry
Welsh Guards	Middlesex Regiment

BENTHEIM

2nd to 3rd April, 1945

In this Engagement, the Irish Guards Group of Guards Armoured Division ran into tough opposition at Gilderhaus. After attacking and clearing this opposition, the Grenadier Group passed through them to fight their way into Bentheim.

The Honour has been awarded to the:-

Life Guards	Irish Guards
Royal Horse Guards	

DREIRWALDE

4th to 8th April, 1945

This Engagement, fought by 52nd Division, involved a strongly-opposed assault across the Dortmund-Ems Canal. It took two days of hard fighting to break through this resistance and capture Dreirwalde.

The Honour was awarded to the:-

Royal Scots Fusiliers	Manchester Regiment
King's Own Scottish Borderers	Highland Light Infantry
Cameronians	King's Royal Rifle Corps

LEESE

5th to 8th April, 1945

In this Engagement, 1st Commando Brigade assaulted across the Weser and met very stiff resistance, being unable to expand its bridgehead. 159th Brigade (11th Armoured Division) crossed well to a flank and took the enemy in rear, when the opposition crumbled.

The Honour is borne on the Colours of the:-   Inns of Court Regiment

and was also awarded to the:-

Rifle Brigade	Commando Association
London Rifle Brigade	

ALLER

10th to 17th April, 1945

In this Engagement, 1st Commando Brigade crossed the river near Essel, secured a bridgehead and beat off two counter-attacks, going on to capture Hademstorf. Meanwhile, 159th Brigade (11th Armoured Division) had captured Winsen. 53rd Division, after two days fighting, capture Rethem and then secured Verden against stiff opposition.

The Honour is borne on the Guidons and Colours of the:-

Royal Scots Greys	East Lancashire Regiment
15th/19th Hussars	Monmouthshire Regiment
Inns of Court Regiment	Herefordshire Light Infantry

and was also awarded to the:-

11th Hussars	King's Royal Rifle Corps

3rd/4th County of London Yeomanry Manchester Regiment
Cheshire Regiment Highland Light Infantry
Royal Welch Fusiliers Rifle Brigade
King's Shropshire Light Infantry Light Rifle Brigade
  Commando Association

BRINKUM

13th to 16th April, 1945.

In this 3rd Division, Engagement, 1/Suffolk captured the cross-roads south-west of Brink, but were forced back by German reinforcements. 185th Brigade attacked round the right flank to capture Brinkum, 1/Suffolk regained the cross-roads, and some 450 prisoners were take in the town.

The Honour was emblazoned by the:-   Suffolk Regiment

And was also awarded to the:-

Royal Warwickshire Regiment East Yorkshire Regiment
Royal Norfolk Regiment Middlesex Regiment

UELZEN

14th to 18th April, 1945.

This Engagement was fought by 15th Division. A dawn attack by 10/H.L.I. on tanks nearly broke into the town. A strong German counter-attach on the Division was beaten off, when the town was cleared.

The Honour was awarded to the:-

Coldstream Guards King's Own Scottish Borderers
Scots Guards Highland Light Infantry
Royal Scots Seaforth Highlanders
Royal Scots Fusiliers Argyll and Sutherland Highlanders

BREMEN

16th to 20th April, 1945

3rd Division, 52nd Division, and 129th Brigade (43rd Division) were concerned in this Engagement. 52nd Division fought their way to the city along the north bank of the Weser, with small fierce battalion fights at Etelsen, Heltebuttel, north of Baden, Uphusen, Borstel, Oyten, and Mahndorf. Then the assaulted Bremen with 43rd Division on their right, while 3rd Division attacked from the south. Resistance was desperate in places, but the main opposition had already been overcome.

The Honour is borne on the Colours of the:-

Royal Scots Greys King's Own Scottish Borderers
Royal Warwickshire Regiment King's Shropshire Light Infantry
Royal Scots Fusiliers Royal Ulster Rifles

and was also awarded to the:-

4th/7th Dragoon Guards Cameronians
13th/18th Hussars Middlesex Regiment
Royal Tank Regiment Wiltshire Regiment
Royal Scots Manchester Regiment

Royal Lincolnshire Regiment
Somerset Light Infantry
South Lancashire Regiment
Highland Light Infantry
East Yorkshire Regiment

ARTLENBERG

29th to 30th April, 1945

In this Engagement, VIII Corps assaulted across the Elbe in L.V.T's., with 1st Commando Brigade, on the right and 44th Brigade (15th Division) on the left. Opposition was light, and the remainder of 15th Division followed. On the 30th April, 11th Armoured Division and 6th Airborne Division began crossing into the bridgehead for the break out next day.

The Honour has been awarded to the:-

Royal Scots
Royal Scots Fusiliers
King's Own Scottish Borderers
Cameronians
Highland Light Infantry
Seaforth Highlanders
Argyll and Sutherland Highlanders

TWENTE CANAL

2nd to 4th April, 1945

This Engagement was primarily the concern of 2nd Canadian Division and 4th Canadian Armoured Division.

The Honour has been awarded to the:- Dorset Regiment

ARNHEM, 1945

12th to 14th April.

In this Engagement, in which 49th Division was involved, 56th Brigade assaulted across the Ijssel in amphibians, the town being subsequently cleared by the rest of the Division. Stiff fighting occurred in places, particularly in the early stages.

The Honour is borne on the Colours of the:- Kensington Regiment

and has also been awarded to the:

Royal Lincolnshire Regiment
South Wales Borderers
York and Lancaster Regiment
Essex Regiment

SOUTHERN FRANCE

15th to 28th August, 1944

This Battle was fought by Seventh U.S. Army, with an Airborne Division containing the British 2nd Parachute Brigade, VI U.S. Corps, and French Army 'B'. The first object was to capture Toulon, and then Marseilles, thereafter to advance north up the Rhone Valley. The airborne Division was dropped in the area Le Muy – Lancers Motte – St. Rosseline – Roquebrunne, on the 15th August, and the garrison of Marseilles surrendered on the 28th August.

The Honour is borne on the Colours of the:-

Glider Pilot Regiment
Parachute Regiment

ABYSSINIA, 1940-41

Although the campaign against Italian East Africa was fought over a vast area, there were few occasions when the numbers engaged amounted to the equivalent of a corps. The campaign was fought under the overall control of General Sir Archibald Wavell, when, as Commander-in-Chief, Middle East, he was fighting the Italians in the Western Desert and Cyrenaica, the Germans in Greece and Crete, and preparing to deal with an insurrection in Iraq and with the French Vichy Forces in Syria. Thus the troops employed were such as could be spared from these other campaigns, and included British, Indian, South African, West African, East African and Sudanese contingents.

The Battles of Keren and the Juba River broke the Italian resistance in the north and south. The Battles of Amba Alagi and Gondar were of almost equal importance in bringing to an end the campaign proper, and the subsequent mopping-up operations.

The results achieved, with comparatively small forces covering great distances, and in the face of numerically superior forces, at a time in the Second World War when the British Armies had not reached their subsequent power in numbers and armaments, account for the comparatively large number of Battle honours that became available for award in this theatre of war.

ABYSSINIA, 1940

This Honour is borne on the Standards of the:-

    Royal Tank Regiment

and has also been awarded to the:-

    Essex Regiment

ABYSSINIA, 1940-41

This Honour is borne on the Colours of the:-

    King's African Rifles   Gold Coast Regiment
    Nigeria Regiment

and has also been awarded to the :-

    West Yorkshire Regiment   Worcestershire Regiment

ABYSSINIA, 1941

This Honour is borne on the Colours of the:-

    Royal Sussex Regiment   Northern Rhodesia Regiment

and has also been awarded to the:-

    Highland Light Infantry   Argyll and Sutherland Highlanders
    Queen's Own Cameron Highlanders

JEBEL DAFEIS

10th January, 1941

This was a successful Engagement, north-east of Metemma, in which the 2nd Battalion, West Yorkshire

Regiment, supported by 389 Field Battery, R.A., attacked an enemy post. After a short resistance the enemy fled, leaving 36 killed.

The Honour has been awarded to the:-
West Yorkshire Regiment

JEBEL SHIBA

21st – 23rd January, 1941

The 10th Indian Infantry Brigade Group, including 2nd, H.L.I, 4th/10th Baluch Regiment and 3rd/18th R. Garhwal Rifles, fought this Engagement with the object of intercepting the Italian retreat from Keru. Six hundred prisoners, and several guns, were taken.

The Honour has been awarded to the:-
Highland Light Infantry

GOGNI

26th January, 1941

This Engagement was the second of three successful attacks against the rearguards of retreating Italian forces on the Barentu Road. Stubborn resistance took 12 hours to overcome. 1st Battalion, Worcestershire Regiment, was the British unit in 29th Indian Infantry Brigade, the other troops taking part being the 3rd/2nd Punjab Regiment, 'B' Troop Sudan Regiment, two troops of artillery and a company of sappers and miners.

The Honour has been awarded to the:-
Worcestershire Regiment

AGORDAT

28th January – 1st February, 1941

This was an Action fought by 4th Indian Division. Contact had been gained with the enemy some 5 miles from Agordat, and it was hoped to outflank him by the seizure of Mt. Cochen. Initial surprise was, however, lost, and when the enemy reinforced Cochen it was decided to carry out a frontal assault up the plain using 'I' Tanks. This was successful, and the enemy only just managed to extricate himself. 2nd Bn., Cameron Highlanders, with 3rd/14th Punjab Regiment and 1st/6th Rajputana Rifles, were in the 11th Indian Infantry Brigade Group, and 1st Royal Fusiliers, with 3rd/1st Punjab Regiment and 4th/11th Sikh Regiment, and 'B' Squadron, 4th Bn., Royal Tank Regiment, were in 5th Indian Infantry Brigade Group.

The Honour has been awarded to the:-
Royal Fusiliers   Queen's Own Cameron Highlanders

BARENTU

27th January – 2nd February, 1941

5th Indian Division, comprising 10th Indian Infantry Brigade Group, (2nd Highland Light Infantry, 4th/10th Baluch Regiment and 3rd/18th Garhwal Regt.), and 29th Indian Infantry Brigade Group, (1st Worcestershire Regt., 3rd/2nd Punjab Regiment and 6th/13th Frontier Force Rifles), fought this Action. 10th Brigade advanced from the north to be held up in the Barentu Gorge, and severe fighting took place.

Meanwhile, 29th Brigade advanced from the west, also meeting considerable opposition, The combined pressure of the two brigades compelled the enemy to withdraw, and the fall of Barentu opened communications along the Via Imperiale to Agordat.

The Honour has been awarded to the:-

    Worcestershire Regiment   Highland Light Infantry

KARORA-MARSA TACLAI

9th – 10th February, 1941

This Engagement, during the advance from the north, resulted in the capture of Karora and the harbour of Marsa Taclai, after some opposition, resulting in two officers and 100 other ranks being taken prisoner.

The Battle Honour has been awarded to the:-

    Royal Sussex Regiment

CUBCUB

23rd February, 1941

This Engagement involved an attack by the 3rd Chad Battalion from the north, and part of the 1st Royal Sussex from the south, which carried out during the advance on Keren. The enemy lost 550 prisoners and four guns

The Honour has been awarded to the:-

    Royal Sussex Regiment

MESCELIT PASS

1st March, 1941

This Engagement was a successful attack, carried out during the advance on Mt. Engiahat, made by 1st Royal Sussex and 4th/16th Punjab Regiment.

The Honour has been awarded to the:-

    Royal Sussex Regiment

KEREN

3rd February-31st March, 1941

The Battle of Keren was the hardest and most prolonged of the Abyssinian Battles. It resulted in over 3,500 British and 10,000 Italian casualties, of which over 3,000 were reckoned killed. It virtually ended the resistance of the Italians in Eritrea and Northern Abyssinia, and deservedly ranks as one of the great Battles of the Second World War.

The Honour is borne on the Colours of the:-

    Royal Fusiliers   Highland Light Infantry
    West Yorkshire Regiment   Queen's Own Cameron Highlanders
    Worcestershire Regiment

and has also been awarded to the:-

    Royal Sussex Regiment

MT. ENGIAHAT

12th to 15th March, 1941

While the main attacks on Keren were made, 7th Indian Infantry Brigade attempted to turn the Italian position from the north. This subsidiary Engagement was not successful, but it pinned down six enemy battalions which would otherwise have been used in the main battle.

The Honour has been awarded to the:-

    Royal Sussex Regiment.

AD TECLESAN

30th to 31st March, 1941

This Engagement, subsidiary to the Battle of Keren, was the last and most important rearguard operation before the Italian withdrawal on Asmara. The enemy were in a strong position, which was frontally attacked by 9th Indian Infantry Brigade, and simultaneously turned by 29th Indian Infantry Brigade. Several hundred prisoners and 67 guns were taken.

The Honour has been awarded to the:-

    West Yorkshire Regiment

MASSAWA

8th April, 1941

This Action disposed of the last resistance made by the Italians in Eritrea.

The attack was carried out by the 7th Indian Infantry Brigade (which included 1st Royal Sussex) from the north, 10th Indian Infantry Brigade, (which included 2nd H.L.I., and 'B' Squadron, 4th R.T.R.) from the west, and the Free French Brigade from the south-west. The 'I' tanks materially assisted in overcoming the opposition, and with the capture by the French of Italian forts the operation was completed, many enemy formations ceasing to exist. 9,590 prisoners, and 127 guns, were captured.

The Honour has been awarded to the:-

    Royal Sussex Regiment   Highland Light Infantry

AMBA ALAGI

20th April to 16th May, 1941

This was the final Battle of the northern campaign, and though only 5th Indian Division and 1st South African Brigade Group were involved, the effect of the campaign as a whole, with the capture of the Italian Viceroy and Commander-in –Chief, the Duke of Aosta, was immense. It resulted in the freeing from Italian domination of the whole of Northern Abyssinia, except for the area round Gondar, and – even more important – in the opening of the road from Addis Ababa to Asmara for the passage of troops.

The Honour has been awarded to the:-

    Worcestershire Regiment

AFODU

9th March, 1941

This was an Engagement on the Blue Nile, involving four successive attacks by 2nd/6th K.A.R., and units of the Sudan Defence Force, on strong defensive positions along the escarpment astride the Asosa-Afodu road,

The Honour has been awarded to the:-

    King's African Rifles

GAMBELA

22nd March, 1941

This Engagement was the culmination of an advance by 2nd/6th K.A.R., and the Belgian Contingent up the Baro River. The eviction of the enemy opened the way into western Galla.

The Honour has been awarded to the:-

    King's African Rifles

MOYALE

1st to 15th July, 1941

The situation of Moyale on the northern boundary of Kenya, and on the only through route from Addis Ababa, made it of importance to both sides. The Italians made two main attacks at this time, between 1st and 3rd July, and 10th and 15th July. The attacks were repulsed by 1st/1st K.A.R.

The Honour for this Engagement has been awarded to the:-

    King's African Rifles

WAL GARIS

10th and 12th September, 1940

In this Engagement on the Kenya border, 3rd G.C. Regt. met the enemy east of the post on 10th September, and inflicted casualties, while 1st G.C. Regt., on 12th September, broke into the enemy position and killed and wounded a number of the enemy. This was the first time 1st G.C. Regt. had been in action as a battalion.

The Honour has been awarded to the:-

    Gold Coast Regiment

EL WAK

15th to 17th December, 1940

This Action was the first operation carried out by General Cunningham with the object of cutting out isolated Italian posts during the period before the rains. 24th (Gold Coast) Infantry Brigade, and 1st South African Infantry Brigade, took part. They completely liquidated the enemy positions; 99 enemy were killed, and 23 prisoners with 15 guns were taken. The success had far-reaching effects on enemy morale.

This Honour is borne on the Colours of the:-

    Gold Coast Regiment

TODENYANG-NAMARAPUTH

9th February, 1941

These two Engagements formed an operation during the advance by 25th East African Brigade on Kalam, in co-operation with 1st South African Division's activities to the east of Lake Rudolf. 2nd/3rd and 2nd/4th K.A.R., with 27 Mountain Battery and armoured cars of the Somaliland Camel Corps, took part.

The Honour has been awarded to the:-

    King's African Rifles

SOROPPA

31st March, 1941

This successful Engagement, fought by 21st East African Brigade, in which 1st/4th K.A.R. carried out an attack on an Italian position, opened the way for the advance on the Lakes by the Dalle Road. Enemy casualties amounted to 50 killed, and over 300 prisoners (including 21 officers, and the Commander of 18 Colonial Brigade) were taken.

The Honour has been awarded to the:-

    King's African Rifles

JUBA

4th to 26th February, 1941

This was the decisive Battle in the south, as Keren was in the north. 11th and 12th African Divisions took part, and, by virtually crushing the Italian resistance in the south, facilitated the advance on Mogadishu and thence to Jijiga and Addis Ababa.

The Honour is borne on the Colours of the:-

    Gold Coast Regiment   King's African Rifles

and has also been awarded to the:-

    Nigeria Regiment

BELES GUGANI

4th February, 1941

This subsidiary Engagement was the first real contact, made by 1st/1st K.A.R., with the enemy in the Juba Battle.

The Honour has been awarded to the:-

    King's African Rifles

BULO ERILLO

13th February, 1941

The main attack in this subsidiary Engagement was made by 2nd G.C. Regt. The enemy, who were heavily entrenched, put up a stout resistance, and 2nd G.C. Regt suffered casualties of 13 killed and 32 wounded. Their fierce attack, however, forced a rapid withdrawal on the enemy, who left his guns behind, besides suffering 207 casualties, including 141 taken prisoner.

The Honour is borne on the Colours of the:-
Gold Coast Regiment

GELIB

21st to 22nd February, 1941

This subsidiary Engagement occurred during the advance by 1st South African Brigade and 24th Gold Coast Brigade, after the crossing of the Juba,

The Honour has been awarded to the:-
Gold Coast Regiment

ALESSANDRA

22nd February, 1941

While 24th Gold Coast Brigade was advancing on Gelib, a small force of 2nd G.C. Regt., with 'A' Company, 1st/3rd K.A.R., and two batteries of light and anti-tank guns, advanced from Bulo Erillo on Alessandra. This subsidiary Engagement resulted from an enemy attack which was repulsed and Alessandra, with much war material, was captured.

The Honour has been awarded to the:-
Gold Coast Regiment

GOLUIN

24th February, 1941

This subsidiary Engagement commemorates the only occasion when Italian rearguards made any resistance between Gelib and Mogadishu. The 1st Nigeria Regt was in a small mixed force which drove the enemy from his mine-covered position before Mogadishu, capturing 5 guns, 8 machine-guns, and a quantity of ammunition.

The Honour has been awarded to the:-
Nigeria Regiment

MARDA PASS

21st to 22nd March, 1941

This Action was fought by 23rd Nigerian Brigade Group after entering the hilly country to the west of Jijiga during the advance from Mogadishu. 1st and 2nd Nigeria Regiment were involved, and inflicted heavy casualties in attacks made against considerable resistance. The fall of the Pass led to the capture of Harar and the final advance on Addis Ababa.

The Honour is borne on the Colours of the:-
Nigeria Regiment

BABILE GAP

23rd to 25th March, 1941

This Engagement took place during the advance to Harar by 23rd Nigerian Brigade, after the capture of the

Marda Pass. The gap is a defile about four miles long through rocky hills, which made progress slow, but an outflanking movement of 1st South African Brigade compelled the enemy to withdraw.

The Honour is borne on the Colours of the:-

Nigeria Regiment

BISIDIMO

26th March, 1941

This Engagement took place at the third rearguard position taken up by the enemy between Jijiga and Harar.

The Honour has been awarded to the:-

Nigeria Regiment

AWASH

2nd and 3rd April, 1941

This Engagement took place at the last of the great natural obstacles to the advance on Addis Ababa. The enemy having destroyed the road and rail bridges, the crossing was made by 22nd East African Brigade. On the 2nd April, 1st/6th K.A.R. drove in the enemy rearguard 8 miles south of the Awash, and 5th K.A.R. forced the river next day. The entry into Addis Ababa followed on the 6th April.

The Honour has been awarded to the:-

King's African Rifles

FIKE

1st May, 1941

The liquidation of the Italians south-west of Addis Ababa began with the advance on the 11th April of 22nd East African Brigade. This Engagement fought by 5th K.A.R. and supporting troops, successfully defeated the enemy holding in some strength a position on Mt. Fike, between Lakes Abyata and Shala, covering the road to Shashamana.

The Honour has been awarded to the:-

King's African Rifles

COLITO

19th May, 1941

On the fall of Shashamana, 22nd East African Brigade turned west to Soddu. This Engagement was fought on finding the enemy holding the Billate river beyond Colito. 1st/6th K.A.R. and 2nd Nigeria Regiment, supported by armoured cars and artillery, took part. The occasion was notable for the bravery of Serjeant N.G. Leakey, K.A.R., who, after the enemy position had been taken, broke single-handed a counter-attack with the tanks which might otherwise have succeeded, and was posthumously awarded the Victoria Cross. Some 100 enemy were killed, as well as over 500 taken prisoner, while 3 tanks and 10 field guns were captured.

The Honour is borne on the Colours of the:-

Nigeria Regiment

and has also been awarded to the:-
King's African Rifles

GIARSO

9th April, 1941

This Engagement took place when 21st East African Brigade, after Soroppa, carried out a reconnaissance towards Giarso, with a view to advancing west of Lake Margherita. This route was found to be held by the enemy, and the force returned to Yavello.

The Honour is borne on the Colours of the:-
Northern Rhodesia Regiment

WADARA

8th April – 10th May, 1941

This Action took place during the advance of 24th Gold Coast Brigade Group from Neghelli. The enemy was found to be holding a strongly entrenched position at Wadara, and prolonged fighting ensued, which took place in thick jungle in the final seven days. Our casualties mounted to 118, while the enemy lost over 1,300.

The Honour is borne on the Colours of the:-
Gold Coast Regiment

OMO

31st May – 6th June, 1941

On the completion of the fighting round the Lakes and the capture of Soddu, General Cunningham decided to advance on Jimma from north-east and south-east. Both these advances entailed the crossing of the Omo River: in the south at Sciola by 22nd East African Brigade, and in the north at Abalti, by 23rd Nigerian Brigade.

Both crossings were held up by floods, but the enemy resistance was badly handled, and soon overcome once the river was crossed. In this Action, over 1,000 prisoners were taken in the south and in the north 2,700, as well as his guns. Our own casualties were light. The crossings over the Omo led to the fall of Jimma and subsequent advances to Didessa and Lechemti, and the eventual surrender of General Gazzera.

The Honour is borne on the Colours of the:-

Nigeria Regiment   King's African Rifles

LECHEMTI

15th June, 1941

This Engagement was fought by 1st Nigeria Regiment and attached troops when 23rd Nigerian Brigade, having turned west after crossing the Omo, encountered a rearguard position east of the River Didessa. For a loss of 6 killed and 8 wounded, 157 enemy were killed and 150 taken prisoner.

The Honour has been awarded to the:-
Nigeria Regiment

GONDAR

15th October to 27th November, 1941

The Battle of Gondar covers the final phase of operations against the remnants of the Italian armies in Abyssinia, ending with the surrender of General Nasi and the fall of the Italian African Empire. 12th African Division and attached forces participated in this Battle.

The Honour is borne on the Colours of the:-

King's African Rifles

AMBAZZO

15th October to 28th November, 1941

This subsidiary Engagement covers operations carried out by 25th and 26th East African Brigades.

The Honour has been awarded to the:-

King's African Rifles

KULKABER

13th and 21st November, 1941

This subsidiary Engagement comprised two attacks, of which the second was the more successful.

The Honour has been awarded to the:-

King's African Rifles

BRITISH SOMALILAND, 1940

The campaign of 14 days was the shortest of the Second World War. It came at a period when the resources in the Middle East theatre were very fully committed, and superiority of numbers available to the enemy in this area could not be adequately countered.

The Italians advanced into British Somaliland in three columns: on Zeila, by the main road Jijiga-Hargeisa-Berbera, and via Odweina.

Total British casualties in the campaign amounted to 260; the enemy admitted to over 2,000.

The theatre honour of 'British Somaliland' is borne on the Colours of the King's African Rifles and the Northern Rhodesia Regiment. It has also been awarded to the:-
>Black Watch

TUG ARGAN
11th to 15th August, 1940

After crossing the frontier and capturing Hargeisa, the enemy made contact with our main forces on 10th August, at the Tug Argan gap. For five days this Action, in which 2nd K.A.R. and 1st N.R.R. were engaged, continued fiercely but inability to prevent outflanking by the enemy made the position untenable. Its loss entailed the loss of the protectorate, and the British forces were ordered to evacuate the country.

The Honour is borne on the colours of the:-
>Northern Rhodesia Regiment

and has also been awarded to the:-
>King's African Rifles

BARKASAN
17th August, 1940

This Engagement was fought by 2nd Black Watch (on whom the brunt of the attack fell) and 2nd K.A.R. to enable the British force to embark at Berbera unmolested. They did well, and inflicted numerous casualties on the enemy.

The Honour has been awarded to the:-
>Black Watch

IRAQ, 1941

2nd to 31st May

This brief campaign became necessary when the pro-Axis Government of Rashid Ali attempted to utilise the period when British Forces in the Middle East were fully committed to other fronts in order to establish enemy air bases in Iraq, and to deny to the British their Treaty right to bring forces into the country in time of war. Hostilities began with the movement of Iraqi ground forces to Habbaniyah, the British Air Force station some 50 miles to the west of Baghdad, and their attempt to invest or overawe the garrison.

The Theatre Honour of 'Iraq, 1941' is borne on the Standards and Guidon of the:

    Life Guards   Warwickshire Yeomanry
    Royal Horse Guards

And has also been awarded to the:-

    Royal Wiltshire Yeomanry   Essex Regiment
    The King's Own Royal Regiment   10th Gurkha Rifles

DEFENCE OF HABBANIYA

2nd to 6th May, 1941

Between 27th and 30th April, some 300 men of 1/King's Own were flown into Habbaniyah from Shaiba. Their night patrols inflicted losses on the enemy during the short siege, and on 6th May, they fought a ground Action which successfully routed the rebels.

The name of this Engagement is borne on the Colours of the:-

    King's Own Royal Regiment

FALLUJA

19th to 22nd May, 1941

This Engagement was fought with the object of capturing the bridge over the Euphrates as a preliminary to advancing on Baghdad. 1/King's Own, 1/Essex, 2/4 Gurkha Rifles, with the support of Assyrian Levies, 237 Battery, R.A., and R.A.F., took part in those operations, in which the enemy suffered heavily before being overcome.

The Honour has been awarded to the:-

    King's Own Royal Regiment   Essex Regiment

BAGHDAD, 1941

28th to 31st May

This was the closing Engagement of the campaign, which forced the river crossings and gave entry to the capital.

The Honour has been awarded to the:-

    Life Guards   Essex Regiment
    Royal Horse Guards

SYRIA, 1941

7th June to 12th July

During the operations in Iraq, German and Italian aircraft had taken part, using air bases in Syria, while the French authorities in the country had supplied arms to the rebels. The Vichy French had, moreover, for some time, been providing a base for enemy propaganda and activities which was no longer tolerable.

7th Australian Division, assisted by Free French troops and part of 1st Cavalry Division, with 5th Indian Infantry Brigade Group comprised the initial force. 6th Division took part in the closing stages of the five weeks' campaign.

The Theatre Honour 'Syria, 1941' is borne on the Standards and Guidons of the:-

    Life Guards
    Royal Horse Guards
    1st Royal Dragoons
    Warwickshire Yeomanry
    Cheshire Yeomanry
    Yorkshire Dragoons
    North Somerset Yeomanry

and has also been awarded to the:-

    Royal Scots Greys
    Royal Wiltshire Yeomanry
    Staffordshire Yeomanry
    Queen's Royal Regiment
    King's Own Royal Regiment
    Royal Fusiliers
    Royal Leicestershire Regiment
    Essex Regiment
    Durham Light Infantry
    10th Gurkha Rifles
    Commando Association

LITANI

9th to 10th June, 1941

This Engagement was a gallantly executed operation, which suffered, however, from faulty planning. No. 11 Commando landed on the beach astride the river in three groups with the object of assisting the coastal advance of the Australians. Severe fighting took place, and part of the Commando, including the headquarters, suffered severe loss.

The Honour was awarded to the:-

    Commando Association

MERJAYUN

9th to 27th June, 1941

This Action includes the initial capture of Merjayun by 25th Australian Infantry Brigade, which then moved on, leaving a small garrison behind. The French recaptured the town a few days later, and were counter-attacked by an Australian force without success

By the 24th June, the Australians, now joined by 2/King's Own, had taken several nearby villages and re-occupied Merjayun

This Honour is borne on the Guidon and Colours of the:-

    Royal Scots Greys
    King's Own Royal Regiment

PALMYRA
21st June to 3rd July, 1941

The airfield at this desert oasis had been subjected to air attack since 8th June, but the activities of the 4th Cavalry Brigade Group were initially unable to eject the French garrison. On 28th June, 1/Essex, arriving from Iraq, established themselves on the height to the north-west of Palmyra and for three days attempted, with the Royal Wiltshire Yeomanry, to penetrate into the town. At last, on 3rd July, the garrison of 187 surrendered.

The Honour for this Action was emblazoned by the:-

Life Guards	Royal Wiltshire Yeomanry
Royal Horse Guards	Essex Regiment

DEIR EZ ZOR
1st to 3rd July, 1941

In the closing stages of the campaign 10th Indian Division began to move from Iraq into Syria. The first objective was the important bridge and track-centre at Deir ez Zor. 21st Indian Brigade Group moved along the Euphrates through Abu Kemal, coming under shellfire from Deir ez Zor by 1st July. On 3rd, two successful attacks were made, resulting in the capture of nine guns and 100 prisoners.

The Honour for this Engagement has been awarded to the:-

10th Gurkha Rifles

JEBEL MAZAR
10th to 12th July, 1941

6th Division was advancing towards Zahle with the object of seizing Rayak airfield and cutting off the Vichy forces on the Merjayun front. The enemy began to offer strong resistance, and it was clear that the heights of the Jebel Mazar (5,000 feet) must first be secured. 2/3rd Australian Battalion made two unsuccessful attempts in the last week of June to do this. On 27th June, supported by 2/Queen's, they were successful but failed to retain their positions. Further attempts were abandoned until the night of the 9th/10th July, when 16th Infantry Brigade attacked, and after heavy and exhausting fighting the end came and with it the surrender of the French Command in Syria.

This Engagement is borne on the Guidon of the:-

North Somerset Yeomanry

And has also been awarded to the:-

King's Own Royal Regiment	Royal Leicestershire Regiment

NORTH AFRICA, 1940 – 43

12th June, 1940 to 12th May, 1943

The campaign opened with the entry of Italy into the war at a time when it appeared that British and French fortunes were lost. It covered the initial advance of Italian forces into Egypt, and their overwhelming defeat and subsequent rout by the Western Desert Force until Lieut.-General Sir Richard O'Connor in the winter of 1940-41; the advance and first withdrawal from Agedabia, and the long defence or Tobruk in 1941; the first offensive by Eighth Army in Operation Crusader in the winter of 1941-42; the second withdrawal from Agedabia, the loss of Tobruk, and the stand on the Alamein Line; the decisive victory at El Alamein in October, 1942, turning point of the war, and the landings in Algeria in that winter by First Army; and the final triumphs in Tripolitania and Tunisia in the spring of 1943.

The Honour 'North Africa, 1940-43,' is borne on the Colours of the:-

    Royal Tank Regiment   Rifle Brigade
    Royal Sussex Regiment   Special Air Service Regiment
    King's Royal Rifle Corps   Sherwood Rangers Yeomanry

and has also been awarded to the:-

    11th Hussars   Royal Hampshire Regiment
    Coldstream Guards   Durham Light Infantry
    Queen's Royal Regiment   Cameron Highlanders
    Royal Northumberland Fusiliers   Argyll and Sutherland Highlanders
    Cheshire Regiment

The Honour 'North Africa, 1940-42' is borne on the Guidon and Colours of the:-

    3rd Hussars   King's Own Royal Regiment
    8th Hussars

and has also been awarded to the:-

    West Yorkshire Regiment   Welch Regiment
    Highland Light Infantry

The Honour 'North Africa, 1940-41, '43' is borne on the Colours of the:-

    Royal Leicestershire Regiment

The Honour 'North Africa, 1940-41' is borne on the Guidon of the:-

    7th Hussars

The Honour 'North Africa, 1940, '43' is borne on the Colours of the:-

    Royal Fusiliers

The Honour 'North Africa, 1940' was emblazoned by the:-

    South Staffordshire Regiment

The Honour 'North Africa, 1941-43' is borne on the Standards, Guidons, Colours and Appointments of the:-

    King's Dragoon Guards   12th Lancers
    Queen's Bays   Scots Guards
    1st Royal Dragoons   Tower Hamlets Rifles

and has also been awarded to the:-

  3rd/4th County of London Yeomanry Buffs
  Honourable Artillery Company Black Watch
  Commando Association Essex Regiment

The Honour 'North Africa, 1941-42' is borne on the Guidon of the:-

  Royal Gloucestershire Hussars

and has also been awarded to the:-

  Worcestershire Regiment

The Honour 'North Africa, 1941, '43' is borne on the Colours of the:-

  Bedfordshire and Hertfordshire Regiment

and has also been awarded to the:-

  York and Lancaster Regiment

The Honour 'North Africa, 1942-43' has been emblazoned by the:-

  Life Guards East Surrey Regiment
  Royal Horse Guards Northamptonshire Regiment
  9th Lancers Gordon Highlanders
  16th/5th Lancers London Irish Rifles
  17th/21st Lancers London Rifle Brigade
  Yorkshire Dragoons Royal Inniskilling Fusiliers
  Lothians and Border Horse

and has also been awarded to the:-

  Royal Scots Greys Duke of Cornwall's Light Infantry
  10th Hussars Sherwood Foresters
  Staffordshire Yeomanry Royal West Kent Regiment
  Derbyshire Yeomanry Middlesex Regiment
  Grenadier Guards Seaforth Highlanders
  East Yorkshire Regiment Parachute Regiment
  Green Howards 2nd Gurkha Rifles
  Lancashire Fusiliers

The Honour 'North Africa, 1942' was emblazoned by the:-

  Warwickshire Yeomanry Rangers
  South Wales Borderers Queen's Westminsters

and has also been awarded to the:-

  4th Hussars 7th Gurkha Rifles
  Royal Wiltshire Yeomanry

The Honour 'North Africa, 1943' was emblazoned by the:-

  Irish Guards Loyal Regiment
  Royal Lincolnshire Regiment North Staffordshire Regiment

and has also been awarded to the:-

  North Irish Horse King's Own Yorkshire Light Infantry
  Welsh Guards King's Shropshire Light Infantry
  Duke of Wellington's Regiment Oxfordshire and Buckinghamshire Light Infantry

EGYPTIAN FRONTIER, 1940

12th June to 12th September

This Action covers the initial period of domination of the frontier area by our light forces, when constant brushes occurred with the enemy, in which losses were inflicted on him.

The Honour has been emblazoned by the:-

    7th Hussars   King's Royal Rifle Corps
    11th Hussars

and has also been awarded to the:-

    8th Hussars   Rifle Brigade
    Coldstream Guards

WITHDRAWAL TO MATRUH

13th to 17th September, 1940

This Engagement involved rearguard Actions by 7th Support Group before the advance of two Italian Corps.

The Honour has been awarded to the:-

    11th Hussars

BIR ENBA

19th November, 1940

A sharp Engagement in which elements of 3rd Hussars, 11th Hussars and 2/R.T.R. routed an enemy force.

The Honour has been awarded to the:-

    11th Hussars

SIDI BARRANI

8th to 11th December, 1940

This was the first Battle of the campaign in North Africa. 7th Armoured Division, 4th Indian Division and the Matruh Garrison, under General O'Connor's direction, gained a brilliant victory, capturing 38,300 prisoners, 237 guns and 73 tanks, and annihilating eight Italian Divisions.

The Honour is borne on the Colours of the:-

    3rd Hussars   Cameron Highlanders
    11th Hussars   Argyll and Sutherland Highlanders
    Coldstream Guards
    Royal Northumberland Fusiliers
    Royal Leicestershire Regiment

and has also been awarded to the:-

    8th Hussars   Cheshire Regiment
    Royal Tank Regiment   South Staffordshire Regiment
    Queen's Royal Regiment   King's Royal Rifle Corps
    Royal Fusiliers

BUQ BUQ
11th December, 1940

This subsidiary Action was emblazoned by the:-
    3rd Hussars   8th Hussars

and was also awarded to the:-
    11th Hussars

BARDIA, 1941
3rd to 5th January

This Battle, fought by XIII Corps, comprising 7th Armoured Division, 6th Australian Division, and 16th Brigade, resulted in the capture of the fortress with 44,800 prisoners, 440 guns, and 130 tanks.

The Honour has been awarded to the:-
    11th Hussars

CAPTURE OF TOBRUK
21st to 22nd January, 1941

In this Battle, 7th Armoured Division and 6th Australian Division captured the fortress with 25,000 prisoners, 200 guns, and 87 tanks.

The Honour is borne on the Colours of the:-
    Cheshire Regiment

and has also been awarded to the:-
    11th Hussars

BEDA FOMM
5th to 8th February, 1941

In this Battle, 7th Armoured Division, after a brilliant desert march to outflank the enemy, annihilated the remnants of the Italian Tenth Army.

The Honour is borne on the Colours of the:-
    King's Dragoon Guards   11th Hussars
    3rd Hussars   Rifle Brigade
    7th Hussars

and has also been awarded to the:-
    Royal Tank Regiment

MERSA EL BREGA
31st March, 1941

In this Engagement, 2nd Special Group fought a rearguard Action against overwhelming enemy superiority.

The Honour is borne on the Colours of the:-
    Tower Hamlets Rifles

and has also been awarded to the:-
    Rifle Brigade

AGEDABIA
2nd April, 1941

2nd Special Group and 3rd Armoured Brigade made a rearguard stand in this Engagement against a superior enemy force.

The Honour has been awarded to the:-

    Rifle Brigade   Tower Hamlets Rifles

DERNA AERODROME
7th April, 1941

This Engagement involved fighting between elements of 2nd Armoured Division and German armoured forces.

The Honour has been awarded to the:-

    King's Royal Rifle Corps   Tower Hamlets Rifles
    Rifle Brigade

HALFAYA, 1941
15th to 27th May

7th Armoured Brigade, 7th Support Group, 22nd Guards Brigade and 4/R.T.R. were involved in this Engagement, during which Halfaya Pass was recaptured and subsequently lost.

The Honour has been awarded to the:-

    11th Hussars   Scots Guard
    Coldstream Guards   Durham Light Infantry

SIDI SULEIMAN
15th to 17th June, 1941

This Action was known as Operation Battleaxe, and had the relief of Tobruk as its object. It was unsuccessful and resulted in the loss of 96 tanks. 4th and 7th Armoured Brigades, with 11th Indian Infantry Brigade (4th Indian Division) and 22nd Guards Brigade took part.

The Honour is borne on the Guidon of the:-

    3rd Hussars

and has been awarded to the:-

    11th Hussars   Scots Guards
    Royal Tank Regiment   Buffs

DEFENCE OF TOBRUK
8th April to 10th December, 1941

This Battle primarily records the successful Australian defence of this fortress, assisted by the Polish Carpathian Brigade and a few British units. In October, 70th Division relieved 9th Australian Division.

The Honour is borne on the standard and Colours of the:-

    King's Dragoon Guards   Royal Northumberland Fusiliers

TOBRUK, 1941

18th November to 10th December

Known as Operation Crusader, this Battle, which began under the command of General Sir Alan Cunningham and ended under command of General Sir Neil Ritchie (as he became later), was remarkable for a vigorous counter-attack by the enemy commander, Rommel, which initially disrupted the plans of the attacking Eighth Army. Dogged fighting overcame the German-Italian resistance, and with the defeat of the enemy Tobruk was relieved by 10th December.

The British forces included XIII Corps (2nd New Zealand Division, 4th Indian Division, 2nd South African Division), XXX Corps (7th Armoured Division and 1st South African Division) and Tobruk Garrison, which broke out from the fortress to take its part in the Battle (70th Division, Polish Brigade, and 32nd Army Tank Brigade).

The Honour is borne on the Colours of the:-

Royal Tank Regiment	Essex Regiment
Royal Gloucestershire Hussars	York and Lancaster Regiment
Coldstream Guards	Durham Light Infantry
Queen's Royal Regiment	Tower Hamlets Rifles
Royal Northumberland Fusiliers	Special Air Service Regiment
Border Regiment	
Black Watch	

and has also been awarded to the:-

King's Dragoon Guards	Bedfordshire and Hertfordshire Regiment
11th Hussars	Royal Leicestershire Regiment
3rd/4th County of London Yeomanry	King's Royal Rifle Corps
Scots Guards	Cameron Highlanders
King's Own Royal Regiment	Rifle Brigade

GUBI I

19th November, 1941

This subsidiary Engagement records an indecisive attack by 22nd Armoured Brigade on the Ariete Division, leading to heavy tank casualties.

The Honour is borne on the Guidon of the:-

Royal Gloucestershire Hussars

and has also been awarded to the:-

11th Hussars	3rd/4th County of London Yeomanry

GABR SALEH

19th to 21st November, 1941

This subsidiary Engagement was the scene of an indecisive clash between 4th and 22nd Armoured Brigades and enemy armour.

The Honour has been awarded to the:-

11th Hussars	3rd/4th County of London Yeomanry

SIDI REZEGH, 1941

19th to 23rd November

In this hard fought subsidiary Action, 7th Armoured Brigade, 7th Support Group, 5th South African Brigade and 6th New Zealand Brigade, were all involved in the defence of the airfield against bitter enemy attacks.

Brigadier J. Campbell, commander of the Support Group, won the V.C. for his gallant leadership here.

This Honour is borne on the Guidons and Appointments of the:-

7th Hussars	3rd/4th County of London Yeomanry
8th Hussars	King's Royal Rifle Corps
11th Hussars	Rifle Brigade
Royal Gloucestershire Hussars	

and has also been awarded to the:-

Royal Tank Regiment

TOBRUK SORTIE

21st to 23rd November

This subsidiary Action was the sortie by 70th Division, and 32nd Army Tank Brigade, from the Fortress to link up with 2nd New Zealand Division at Belhamed.

The Honour is borne on the Colours of the:-

King's Own Royal Regiment	Bedfordshire and Hertfordshire Regiment

and has also been awarded to the:-

King's Dragoon Guards	Black Watch
Queen's Royal Regiment	York and Lancaster Regiment

OMARS

22nd November to 2nd December, 1941

Successful attacks on enemy positions by 4th Indian Division in the area of the Omars were made in this subsidiary Action. 42/R.T.R., with 5th and 7th Indian Infantry Brigades and 5th New Zealand Brigade, took part.

The Honour is borne on the Colours of the:-

Royal Sussex Regiment

TAIEB EL ESSEM

24th to 25th November, 1941

4th Armoured Brigade and 1st South African Brigade successfully defended this area against German armoured forces in this subsidiary Engagement.

The Honour was awarded to the:-

11th Hussars

BELHAMED

25th November to 1st December, 1941

In this subsidiary Action 70th Division, 2nd New Zealand Division, 7th Armoured Division and 1st South African Brigade, were involved in operations leading to the establishment of the southern end of the corridor from Tobruk.

The Honour was emblazoned by the:-

    Bedfordshire and Hertfordshire Regiment

and has also been awarded to the:-

    Royal Tank Regiment   Royal Northumberland Fusiliers
    Essex Regiment

GUBI II

4th to 6th December, 1941

This subsidiary Engagement was an unsuccessful attempt by 7th Armoured Division, and 11th Indian Brigade, to overcome the enemy's position in the vicinity of El Gubi.

The Honour has been awarded to the:-

    11th Hussars   Cameron Highlanders

RELIEF OF TOBRUK

7th to 10th December, 1941

This subsidiary Action formed the closing stages of the Battle of Tobruk, 1941, and included fighting by elements of Eighth Army on the general line Bir el Gubi – Tobruk.

The Honour has been awarded to the:-

    King's Dragoon Guards   11th Hussars
    8th Hussars   Durham Light Infantry

ALEM HAMZA

14th to 16th December, 1941

This was an Action involving an attack by XIII corps on the enemy's positions at Gazala during the pursuit.

The Honour was emblazoned by the:-

    Buffs

CHOR ES SUFAN

27th to 30th December, 1941

This Engagement was the scene of an attempt by 22nd Armoured Brigade to turn the eastern flank of the enemy's position at Agedabia.

The Honour is borne on the Guidons of the:-

    12th Lancers   Royal Gloucestershire Hussars

and has also been awarded to the:-

    3rd/4th County of London Yeomanry   Tower Hamlets Rifles
    Rifle Brigade

SAUNNU

23rd January, 1942

The enemy counter-offensive had begun on 21st January, when 200th Guards Brigade and 1st Support Group were engaged. On the 23rd the armour of 1st Armoured Division became involved, and this Action was a confused melee during the desert withdrawal.

The Honour is borne on the Guidon of the:-

    10th Hussars

and has also been awarded to the:-

    9th Lancers   Rifle Brigade
    11th Hussars

MSUS

25th January, 1942

This Engagement consisted mainly in the clash of small British columns with advancing enemy forces.

The Honour has been awarded to the:-

    Queen's Bays   11th Hussars
    Royal Dragoons   Coldstream Guards

BENGHAZI

27th to 29th January, 1942

This Engagement primarily concerns the break-out by columns of 7th Indian Infantry Brigade, when the town was cut off during the enemy's advance.

The Honour has been awarded to the:-

    Royal Sussex Regiment   Welch Regiment

CARMUSA

29th January to 5th February, 1942

This Engagement covers the withdrawal by 4th Indian Division through the Jebel with fighting at various places, including Carmusa.

The Honour has been awarded to the:-

    Cameron Highlanders

GAZALA

26th May to 21st June, 1942

In this Battle, the Eighth Army, holding the Gazala line, was attacked by German-Italian forces under

Rommel, and after very severe fighting and fluctuating fortunes was forced to withdraw to the frontier defences. 1st and 7th Armoured Divisions, 1st and 32nd Army Tank Brigades, 50th Division, 5th and 10th Indian Divisions, and 1st and 2nd South African Divisions took part.

The Honour is borne on the Guidons and Colours of the:-

Bays	East Yorkshire Regiment
8th Hussars	Green Howards
9th Lancers	Worcestershire Regiment
10th Hussars	Duke of Cornwall's Light Infantry
12th Lancers	Sherwood Foresters
Royal Gloucestershire Hussars	Tower Hamlets Rifles
Scots Guards	

and has also been awarded to the:-

1st King's Dragoon Guards	King's Royal Rifle Corps
Royal Dragoons	Durham Light Infantry
4th Hussars	Highland Light Infantry
Royal Tank Regiment	Cameron Highlanders
3rd/4th County of London Yeomanry	Rifle Brigade
Cheshire Regiment	Rangers
South Wales Borderers	

RETMA

27th May, 1942

In this subsidiary Engagement, part of 7th Motor Brigade was overrun by the advancing enemy.

This Honour is borne on the Appointments of the:-   Rangers

BIR EL IGELA

27th May, 1942

4th Armoured Brigade was the first British armoured formation to be engaged by the enemy during the Battle of Gazala, and in this subsidiary Engagement was forced to withdraw after heavy casualties.

The Honour has been awarded to the:-   8th Hussars

BIR EL ASLAGH

27th to 31st May, 1942

The first real armoured clash of the Battle of Gazala, leading to the withdrawal of the enemy armoured formations, took place in this subsidiary Action.

The Honour was borne on the Guidon of the:-

Royal Gloucestershire Hussars

and has also been awarded to the:-

Queen's Bays	10th Hussars
9th Lancers	

BIR HACHEIM
27th to 11th June, 1942

This subsidiary Action primarily concerned the successful defence of the Bir Hacheim 'Box', until the Free French Brigade holding it was withdrawn. A good deal of fighting took place in the surrounding desert by units endeavouring to assist the garrison.

The Honour is borne on the Appointments of the:-
    Rangers

and has also been awarded to the:-
    King's Dragoon Guards   King's Royal Rifle Corps

CAULDRON
5th to 6th June, 1942

In this subsidiary Action, there was a disastrous ending to the British counter-attack on the enemy forces driven into the desert area known as 'The Cauldron'.

The Honour is borne on the Guidon and Colours of the:-
    Royal Gloucestershire Hussars   Highland Light Infantry
    Royal Northumberland Fusiliers

and has also been awarded to the:-
    Queen's Bays   West Yorkshire Regiment
    Royal Tank Regiment
    3rd/4th County of London Yeomanry

KNIGHTSBRIDGE
6th to 7th June, and 11th to 13th June, 1942

This subsidiary Engagement primarily concerned the successful defence of the Knightsbridge 'Box' by 201st Guards Brigade, until the latter was withdrawn.

The Honour was emblazoned by the:-
    Royal Dragoons
    Honourable Artillery Company

and has also been awarded to the:-
    Queen's Bays   Coldstream Guards
    Royal Tank Regiment   Scots Guards
    King's Royal Rifle Corps   Rifle Brigade

HAGIAG ER RAML
11th to 13th June, 1942

This subsidiary Action was an unsuccessful attempt by all the then remaining British armoured formations, and the garrison of the Knightsbridge and other 'boxes' in the area to halt the enemy counter-attack which led to the final overthrow of the British armour.

The Honour has been awarded to the:-
    3rd/4th County of London Yeomanry

GABR EL FACHRI
14th June, 1942

The break-out of 50th Division from the Gazala Line is commemorated in this subsidiary Engagement.

The Honour has been awarded to the:-
    Durham Light Infantry

VIA BALBIA
14th June, 1942

Operations at a number of localities on the top of the escarpment by British and South African forces are included in this subsidiary Engagement.

The Honour has been awarded to the:-
    Queen's Bays   Worcestershire Regiment

ZT EL MRASSES
15th June, 1942

This subsidiary Engagement was a rearguard operation to break through to Tobruk.

The Honour has been awarded to the:-
    Durham Light Infantry

SIDI REZEGH, 1942
17th June

4th Armoured Brigade unsuccessfully attempted to support 20th Indian Infantry Brigade Group at Belhamed in this subsidiary Engagement.

The Honour has been awarded to the:-
    9th Lancers

TOBRUK, 1942
20th to 21st June

The surrender of Tobruk took place in this subsidiary Action. But some gallant regimental history was made in an otherwise sad record.

The Honour is borne on the Colours and Appointments of the:-
    Coldstream Guards   7th Gurkha Rifles

and has also been awarded to the:-
    Cameron Highlanders

MERSA MATRUH
26th to 30th June, 1942

In this Battle, the enemy forces broke through between X and XIII Corps, cutting off the former in Mersa

Matruh. XIII Corps retired, and the position was not stabilized till the El Alamein line held by XXX Corps was reached.

The Honour has been awarded to the:-

Queen's Bays	Cheshire Regiment
8th Hussars	Essex Regiment
3rd/4th County of London Yeomanry	Durham Light Infantry
East Yorkshire Regiment	Highland Light Infantry

POINT 174
27th June, 1942

This subsidiary Engagement was fought by 9/D.L.I. in an attempt to hold up the enemy advance. Private A. H. Wakenshaw was posthumously awarded the Victoria Cross for conspicuous courage in manning his anti-tank gun.

The Honour has been awarded to the:-

Durham Light Infantry

MINQAR QAIM
27th to 28th June, 1942

In this subsidiary Action 1st British Armoured Division were involved with 2nd New Zealand Division. The latter charged through the enemy lines at night to avoid encirclement.

The Honour has been awarded to the:-

3rd/4th County of London Yeomanry

FUKA
28th June, 1942

A running fight by elements of 29th Indian Infantry Brigade, holding the escarpment west of Fuka, took place in this subsidiary Engagement.

The Honour has been awarded to the:-

Highland Light Infantry

DEFENCE OF ALAMEIN LINE
1st to 27th July, 1942

The fighting in this Battle was heavy and continuous. General Sir Claude Auchinleck, Commander-in-Chief, Middle East, took personal command of the Eighth Army, and not only halted Rommel's Army but by persistent attacks forced the enemy on to the defensive. By the end of the month, though both sides were exhausted, the initiative had passed to the British.

The Honour is borne on the Standard and Colours of the:-

King's Dragoon Guards	Essex Regiment
West Yorkshire Regiment	Tower Hamlets Rifles

and has also been awarded to the:-

Royal Dragoons	East Yorkshire Regiment
4th Hussars	Green Howards
9th Lancers	Cheshire Regiment
11th Hussars	King's Royal Rifle Corps
Royal Tank Regiment	Rifle Brigade
3rd/4th County of London Yeomanry	Rangers
Coldstream Guards	
Scots Guards	

DEIR EL SHEIN

1st July, 1942

In this subsidiary Action 1st Armoured Division and 18th Indian Infantry Brigade Group brought the enemy advance to a halt, although their gallant defence ended with the destruction of the Brigade Group.

The Honour has been awarded to the:-

3rd/4th County of London Yeomanry	Cheshire Regiment
	Essex Regiment

RUWEISAT

2nd to 4th July, 1942

Counter-attacks launched by XIII and XXX Corps, in which units of 1st Armoured Division, 2nd New Zealand Division, 1st South African Division, and columns from 7th Motor Brigade and 5th Indian Division, took part, contributed in this subsidiary Action to defeat advancing enemy forces.

The Honour is borne on the Guidons of the:-

4th Hussars	9th Lancers

and has also been awarded to the:-

3rd/4th County of London Yeomanry	King's Royal Rifle Corps
Essex Regiment	Rifle Brigade
	Rangers

FUKA AIRFIELD

7th July, 1942

This subsidiary Engagement was a successful raid on installations many miles behind the enemy's main positions.

The Honour is borne on the Appointments of the:-

Rangers

and has also been awarded to the:-

King's Royal Rifle Corps

POINT 93
11th July, 1942

2nd Armoured Brigade repulsed an advance by enemy armour in this subsidiary Engagement.

The Honour has been awarded to the:-

    3rd/4th County of London Yeomanry

RUWEISAT RIDGE
14th to 16th July, 1942

In this subsidiary Action, 2nd New Zealand Division, with 5th Indian Infantry Brigade, and 2nd Armoured Brigade, recaptured a part of this feature.

The Honour has been awarded to the:-

9th Lancers	Essex Regiment
3rd/4th County of London Yeomanry	
Royal Northumberland Fusiliers	

ALAM EL HALFA
30th August to 7th September, 1942

This Battle was the final attempt by Rommel to break through to the Delta, and Montgomery's first Battle as Eighth Army commander. The troops involved included 7th and 10th Armoured Divisions, 44th Division, 2nd New Zealand Division, 20th Australian Infantry Brigade, and 9th Indian Infantry Brigade.

The Honour is borne on the Guidons and Colours of the:-

Royal Scots Greys	Royal Gloucestershire Hussars
4th Hussars	3rd/4th County of London Yeomanry
Sherwood Rangers Yeomanry	Royal Sussex Regiment
Staffordshire Yeomanry	King's Royal Rifle Corps
Derbyshire Yeomanry	Rifle Brigade

and has also been awarded to the:-

King's Dragoon Guards	12th Lancers
8th Hussars	Royal Tank Regiment
10th Hussars	Buffs
11th Hussars	Royal West Kent Regiment
	London Rifle Brigade

WEST POINT 23
1st September, 1942

This subsidiary Engagement comprised a diversionary attack made by 20th Australian Infantry Brigade with armoured support.

The Honour is borne on the Guidon of the:-

    Royal Gloucestershire Hussars

BENGHAZI RAID

13th to 14th September, 1942

In this Engagement, a force of S.A.S. troops from Kufra under Lt.-Col. Stirling, made an unsuccessful raid on Benghazi, and suffered heavy casualties.

The Honour has been awarded to the:-

    Special Air Service Regiment

DEIR EL MUNASIB

30th September, 1942

This Action was a 'set piece' attack by 131st Brigade (44th Division) supported by a large concentration of artillery.

The Honour has been awarded to the:-

    Queen's Royal Regiment

EL ALAMEIN

23rd October to 4th November, 1942

This Battle, a 'set piece' attack by Eighth Army, ended with the rout of the German-Italian forces, and was the turning point of the war in North Africa.

The Honour is borne on the Standards, Guidons and Colours of the:-

Life Guards	Queen's Royal Regiment
Royal Horse Guards	Buffs
Queen's Bays	Royal Northumberland Fusiliers
Royal Dragoons	East Yorkshire Regiment
Royal Scots Greys	Green Howards
3rd Hussars	Cheshire Regiment
4th Hussars	Royal Sussex Regiment
8th Hussars	Black Watch
9th Lancers	Sherwood Foresters
10th Hussars	Royal West Kent Regiment
11th Hussars	Middlesex Regiment
12th Lancers	King's Royal Rifle Corps
Royal Tank Regiment	Durham Light Infantry
Royal Wiltshire Yeomanry	Seaforth Highlanders
Warwickshire Yeomanry	Gordon Highlanders
Sherwood Rangers Yeomanry	Cameron Highlanders
Staffordshire Yeomanry	Argyll and Sutherland Highlanders
Yorkshire Dragoons	Rifle Brigade
Derbyshire Yeomanry	2nd Gurkha Rifles
3rd/4th County of London Yeomanry	Queen's Westminsters
Honourable Artillery Company	London Rifle Brigade

and has also been awarded to the:-

    Essex Regiment

CAPTURE OF HALFAYA PASS

10th to 11th November, 1942

In this Engagement, 21st New Zealand Battalion, with assistance from 1KRRC and sappers of 21st Field Squadron, Royal Engineers, captured the Pass by bold action, taking over 6500 Italian prisoners.

The Honour has been awarded to the:-

    King's Royal Rifle Corps

EL AGHEILA

13th to 17th December, 1942

In this Engagement, 2nd New Zealand Division with 4th Light Armoured Brigade, outflanked the enemy position at El Agheila and forced him to flee westwards.

This Honour is borne on the Standard and Guidon of the:-

King's Dragoon Guards	Staffordshire Yeomanry

and has also been awarded to the:-

Royal Dragoons	Sherwood Rangers Yeomanry
Royal Scots Greys	Buffs

NOFILIA

17th to 18th December, 1942

This Engagement arose from the movement of 2nd New Zealand Division, and 4th Light Armoured Brigade, round the southern flank of the Agheila position in the endeavour to block the enemy escape westwards.

This Honour is borne on the Guidon of the:-

    Royal Scots Greys

and has also been awarded to the:-

    King's Royal Rifle Corps

ADVANCE ON TRIPOLI

15th to 23rd January, 1943

This Action, culminating in the capture of Tripoli, was a series of small fights by two columns, one of which advanced along the coast and the other well to the south. 7th Armoured Division, 22nd Armoured Brigade, 51st Division and 2nd New Zealand Division took part.

The Honour is borne on the Standard and Guidons of the:-

King's Dragoon Guards	Sherwood Rangers Yeomanry
Royal Dragoons	Staffordshire Yeomanry

and has also been awarded to the:-

Royal Scots Greys	Buffs
11th Hussars	Royal Northumberland Fusiliers
12th Lancers	Black Watch

Queen's Royal Regiment	Middlesex Regiment
	Seaforth Highlanders
	Gordon Highlanders

MEDENINE

6th March, 1943

This Battle took place during the pursuit by Eighth Army after the capture of Tripoli. Before it was possible to mount an attack on the Mareth line, the enemy launched an unsuccessful offensive against the southern flank.

The Honour is borne on the Colours of the:-

    Scots Guards   Queen's Royal Regiment

and has also been awarded to the:-

    Coldstream Guards   Argyll and Sutherland Highlanders
    Royal Northumberland Fusiliers   Black Watch

ZEMLET EL LEBENE

6th March, 1943

This subsidiary Action was the repulse of the enemy attack on the front of 131st Brigade (7th Armoured Division).

The Honour has been awarded to the:-

    Black Watch

TADJERA KHIR

6th March, 1943

This subsidiary Action was the repulse of the enemy on the front of 201st Guards Brigade.

The Honour has been awarded to the:-

    Scots Guards

MARETH

16th to 23rd March, 1943

In this Battle a frontal attack made by XXX Corps was only partially successful, and there was severe fighting.

The Honour is borne on the Colours of the:-

    Grenadier Guards   Cheshire Regiment
    East Yorkshire Regiment   Durham Light Infantry
    Green Howards   Gordon Highlanders

and has also been awarded to the:-

    Royal Tank Regiment
    Coldstream Guards
    Black Watch   Seaforth Highlanders
    Middlesex Regiment   Cameron Highlanders
          2 Gurkha Rifles

WADI ZEUSS EAST

16th to 17th March, 1943

In this subsidiary Engagement, fought by 50th Division, enemy outposts were driven in and forward positions established.

The Honour has been awarded to the:-

    Cheshire Regiment

WADI ZIGZAOU

20th to 23rd March, 1943

In this subsidiary Action 50th and 51st Divisions were involved in a frontal attack across the Wadi, which failed after severe fighting.

The Honour has been awarded to the:-

East Yorkshire Regiment	Seaforth Highlanders
Cheshire Regiment	Cameron Highlanders

TEBAGA GAP

21st to 30th March, 1943

This Battle, fought mainly by the New Zealand Division with 1st Armoured Division, carried out a 'Left Hook,' defeated the enemy in the Tebaga Gap, and pursued them to Gabes.

The Honour is emblazoned by the:-

King's Dragoon Guards	Staffordshire Yeomanry
Sherwood Rangers Yeomanry	London Rifle Brigade

and has also been awarded to the:-

Queen's Bays	Yorkshire Dragoons
9th Lancers	Buffs
12th Lancers	King's Royal Rifle Corps
	Rifle Brigade

POINT 201 (ROMAN WALL)

21st to 22nd March, 1943

This subsidiary Action, in which 6th New Zealand Brigade were mainly involved, was the capture of an enemy outpost position.

The Honour has been awarded to the:-

King's Dragoon Guards	Staffordshire Yeomanry
Sherwood Rangers Yeomanry	

EL HAMMA

27th to 29th March, 1943

This subsidiary Action was fought by 1st Armoured Division during the pursuit.

The Honour is borne on the standard and Guidons of the:-

    Queen's Bays
    9th Lancers
    10th Hussars
    Yorkshire Dragoons
    Honourable Artillery Company

and has also been awarded to the:-

    King's Dragoon Guards
    12th Lancers
    Sherwood Rangers Yeomanry
    Staffordshire Yeomanry
    Buffs

MATMATA HILLS

25th to 28th March, 1943

In this Engagement, 4th Indian Division carried out operations to open communications with the New Zealand Division.

The Honour has been awarded to the:-

    Essex Regiment

AKARIT

6th to 7th April, 1943

This Battle, in which X and XXX Corps of Eighth Army took part, did not sufficiently succeed on the first day to enable a break-through. By the early hours of the 7th, the enemy had evacuated his positions.

The Honour is emblazoned by the:-

    Staffordshire Yeomanry
    Green Howards
    Royal Sussex Regiment
    Black Watch
    Seaforth Highlanders
    Cameron Highlanders
    Argyll and Sutherland Highlanders
    2nd Gurkha Rifles

and has also been awarded to the:-

    King's Dragoon Guards
    12th Lancers
    Royal Tank Regiment
    3rd/4th County of London Yeomanry
    Buffs
    East Yorkshire Regiment
    Cheshire Regiment
    Essex Regiment
    Middlesex Regiment

DJEBEL EL MEIDA

6th April, 1943

In this subsidiary Action, 7th Indian Infantry Brigade opened the Battle by overrunning the enemy's forward posts, capturing the Mesreb el Alig feature, and exploiting eastwards to Djebel el Meida.

The Honour has been awarded to the:-

    Royal Sussex Regiment
    2nd Gurkha Rifles

WADI AKARIT EAST

6th to 7th April, 1943

This subsidiary Action was the attack by 154th Brigade (51st Division).

The Honour has been awarded to the:-

    Cheshire Regiment   Black Watch

DJEBEL ROUMANA

6th to 7th April, 1943

This subsidiary Action was the attack by 152nd Brigade (51st Division).

The Honour has been awarded to the:-

    3rd/4th County of London Yeomanry   Middlesex Regiment
    Black Watch   Seaforth Highlanders
                                                          Cameron Highlanders

SEBKRET EN NOUAL

7th April, 1943

8th Armoured Brigade repulsed an attack by enemy tanks in this Engagement.

The Honour has been awarded to the:-

    Staffordshire Yeomanry

CHEBKET EN NOUIGES

8th April, 1943

8th Armoured Brigade checked an attempt by enemy tanks to outflank them in this Engagement.

The Honour has been awarded to the:-

    Sherwood Rangers Yeomanry

DJEBEL EL TELIL

9th April, 1943

In this Engagement, enemy armour sought to delay the advance of 2nd and 8th Armoured Brigades, and 2nd New Zealand Division.

The Honour has been awarded to the:-

    Staffordshire Yeomanry

ENFIDAVILLE

19th to 29th April, 1943

In this Battle, the main thrust was made by 2nd New Zealand Division and the 4th Indian Division, but both divisions got held up. 50th Division advanced on the right flank, and 7th Armoured Division protected the left flank.

The Honour is borne on the Guidon and Colours of the:-

    Staffordshire Yeomanry   Essex Regiment
    Oxfordshire and Buckinghamshire Light Infantry

and has also been awarded to the:-

    11th Hussars   Cheshire Regiment
    Sherwood Rangers Yeomanry   2nd Gurkha Rifles

TAKROUNA

20th to 21st April, 1943

This subsidiary Action was mainly fought by 2nd New Zealand Division.

The Honour has been awarded to the:-

    Sherwood Rangers Yeomanry   Staffordshire Yeomanry

DJEBEL GARCI

20th April, 1943

Hard fighting by 4th Indian Division took place in this subsidiary Action.

The Honour has been awarded to the:-

    Essex Regiment.

DJEBEL TEBAGA

8th to 9th May, 1943

In this Engagement an abortive attempt to cut the coast road by capturing this feature was made by 169th Brigade (56th Division).

The Honour has been awarded to the:-

    Royal Fusiliers.

DJEBEL ABIOD

17th November, 1942

The first clash by elements of First Army with the enemy in North Africa occurred in this Engagement, when the German advance westward was checked.

The Honour has been awarded to the:-

    Royal West Kent Regiment.

SOUDIA

24th November, 1942

In this Engagement, 1/Parachute Battalion attacked an enemy position.

The Honour has been awarded to the:-

    Parachute Regiment.

MEDJEZ EL BAB

25th to 26th November, 1942

11th Infantry Brigade (78th Division) and 'Bladeforce' – an improvised column of armour and infantry – undertook operations of varying success in this Action.

The Honour is borne on the Guidon and Colours of the:-

    Derbyshire Yeomanry   Lancashire Fusiliers

and has also been awarded to the:-

    Rifle Brigade

TEBOURBA

27th November, 1942

A successful defence against strong German tank attack took place in this Engagement, fought by 11th Infantry Brigade with elements of 78th Division.

The Honour has been awarded to the:-

    East Surrey Regiment

DJEDEIDA

28th to 29th November, 1942

In this Engagement, the British advance on Tunis was halted by the enemy.

The Honour has been awarded to the:-

    Northamptonshire Regiment

DJEBEL AZZAG, 1942

28th to 30th November

In this Action, our advance on Mateur was halted by the enemy after severe fighting.

The Honour has been awarded to the:-

    Royal West Kent Regiment   Argyll and Sutherland Highlanders

OUDNA

29th November to 34d December, 1942

In this Engagement, 2/Parachute Battalion was dropped at Depienne to attack Oudna airfield, afterwards making a fighting withdrawal to Medjez el Bab.

The Honour is borne on the Colours of the:-

    Parachute Regiment

TEBOURBA GAP

1st to 10th December, 1942

This Battle occurred when a very heavy counter-offensive was launched from the east and north against

Tebourba and the Tebourba Gap. 11th Infantry Brigade Group and 'Bladeforce' were forced to withdraw suffering heavy losses in men and equipment.

The Honour is borne on the Guidon and Colours of the:-

    17th/21st Lancers   Royal Hampshire Regiment

and has also been awarded to the:-

    Derbyshire Yeomanry

LONGSTOP HILL, 1942

23rd to 25th December

In this Action, 1st Guards Brigade, after heavy fighting, failed to capture this feature during the renewed advance on Tunis.

The Honour has been awarded to the:-

    Coldstream Guards

DJEBEL AZZAG, 1943

5th to 7th January

This Action was an unsuccessful attack on an enemy position.

The Honour has been awarded to the:-

    Buffs   Parachute Regiment

TWO TREE HILL

13th January, 1943

This Engagement was an unsuccessful attack by 26th Armoured Brigade and attached troops, on this and neighbouring heights.

The Honour has been awarded to the:-

    Royal Inniskilling Fusiliers

BOU ARADA

18th to 25th January, 1943

This was an Allied Battle involving British, American and French forces. The German offensive launched on 18th January, was held on the front of 6th Armoured Division, but broke through the French front. 36th and 38th Infantry Brigade of 78th Division, also took part.

The Honour is borne on the Appointments of the:-

    Royal Irish Fusiliers
    London Irish Rifles

and has also been awarded to the:-

    17th/21st Lancers   Lothians and Border Horse
    Derbyshire Yeomanry   Royal Inniskilling Fusiliers

ROBAA VALLEY
31st January, 1943

In this Engagement, a German tank attack was defeated by 36th Brigade.

The Honour is borne on the Colours of the:-
    Buffs

DJEBEL ALLILIGA
3rd to 4th February, 1943

This Engagement involved an unsuccessful assault on the Djebel Mansour – Djebel Alliliga position by 1st Guards Brigade, 1st Parachute Battalion and French forces.

The Honour has been awarded to the:-
    Parachute Regiment

KASSERINE
14th to 25th February, 1943

6th Armoured Division and 1st Guards Brigade, together with French forces, took part in this Battle, which began with forward elements of 2nd United States Corps being thrown back by the enemy. The latter advanced until checked at Sbiba and Thala, when he withdrew.

The Honour is emblazoned by the:-

17th/21st Lancers	Lothians and Border Horse

and has also been awarded to the:-

16th/5th Lancers	Rifle Brigade
Derbyshire Yeomanry	Tower Hamlets Rifles

SBIBA
19th to 22nd February, 1943

In this subsidiary Action, 1st Guards Brigade and attached troops successfully halted the German drive northwards.

The Honour has been awarded to the:-

Honourable Artillery Company	Coldstream Guards

THALA
20th to 22nd February, 1943

26th Armoured Brigade and attached troops successfully halted the German drive westwards in this subsidiary Action.

The Honour was emblazoned by the:-

Honourable Artillery Company	Tower Hamlets Rifles

and has also been awarded to the:-

17th/21st Lancers	Rifle Brigade
Lothians and Border Horse	

EL HADJEBA

26th February, 1943

In this Engagement, the position held by 3rd Parachute Battalion was lost, and recovered by counter-attack.

The Honour has been awarded to the:-

    Parachute Regiment   London Irish Rifles

DJEBEL DJAFFA

26th February, 1943

11th Brigade was involved in this Engagement.

The Honour has been awarded to the:-

    Northamptonshire Regiment

SIDI NSIR

26th February, 1943

In this Engagement, the outpost position of 128th Brigade (46th Division) was overrun after a gallant defence.

The Honour has been awarded to the:-

    Royal Hampshire Regiment

FORT McGREGOR

26th to 27th February, 1943

This Engagement involved the loss and recapture of the Lalla Manna areas.

The Honour has been awarded to the:-

    East Surrey Regiment

STUKA FARM

26th to 28th February, 1943

38th Brigade, in this Engagement, lost and recaptured Castle Hill and Stuka Farm.

The Honour has been awarded to the:-

    Royal Irish Fusiliers
    London Irish Rifles

STEAMROLLER FARM

26th February to 1st March, 1943

In this Engagement, the enemy's advance via Tally Ho Corner and El Aroussa, was repulsed with heavy loss.

The Honour has been awarded to the:-

    Derbyshire Yeomanry   Coldstream Guards
                                           Commando Association

HUNT'S GAP

27th to 28th February, 1943

In this Action of 128th Brigade, the enemy was checked with heavy loss in tanks.

The Honour is borne on the Guidon and Colours of the:-

    North Irish Horse   Royal Hampshire Regiment

MONTAGNE FARM

28th February to 2nd March, 1943

Considerable fighting took place in this Engagement.

The Honour has been awarded to the:-

    Royal Leicestershire Regiment   Royal Hampshire Regiment

KEF OUIBA PASS

28th February to 4th March, 1943

In this Engagement the position was lost, but regained after considerable fighting.

The Honour has been awarded to the:-

    Argyll and Sutherland Highlanders

DJEBEL GUERBA

2nd March, 1943

In this Engagement an attack on the enemy position failed with heavy losses.

The Honour has been awarded to the:-

    Sherwood Foresters

SEDJENANE I

4th March, 1943

139th Brigade (46th Division) and attached troops were forced to retire from Sedjenane in this Engagement.

The Honour has been awarded to the:-

    North Irish Horse   Durham Light Infantry
    Royal Lincolnshire Regiment   Commando Association

TAMERA

5th to 15th March, 1943

In this Action, 139th Brigade and 1st Parachute Brigade were forced to retire from the Tamera position.

The Honour is borne on the Colours of the:-

    Parachute Regiment

and has also been awarded to the:-

    North Irish Horse   Sherwood Foresters

MAKNASSY
12th to 31st March, 1943

In this Engagement, 1st Derby Yeo. Were operating with II U.S. Corps.

The Honour has been awarded to the:-
  Derbyshire Yeomanry

DJEBEL DAHRA
20th to 24th March, 1943

In this Engagement, the position lost on 20th March was finally regained on the 24th.

The Honour has been awarded to the:-
  Parachute Regiment

DJEBEL CHOUCHA
28th March, 1943

In this Action, 36th Brigade and No 1 Commando captured the feature.

The Honour has been awarded to the:-
  Commando Association

KEF EL DEBNA
28th March, 1943

1st Parachute Brigade and attached troops captured this locality in this Action.

The Honour has been awarded to the:-
  Parachute Regiment

MINE DE SEDJENANE
30th to 31st March, 1943

138th Brigade occupied the position in this Engagement after overcoming obstinate resistance.

The Honour was emblazoned by the:-
  York and Lancaster Regiment

and has also been awarded to the:-
  Royal Lincolnshire Regiment   Argyll and Sutherland Highlanders
  King's Own Yorkshire Light Infantry

FONDOUK
7th to 11th April, 1943

The operations in this Battle, in which IX Corps and U.S. forces took part, were intended to break through the Fondouk Pass and cut the enemy communications in the Kairouan area.

The Honour is borne on the Guidons and Colours of the:-

16th/5th Lancers
17th/21st Lancers
Welsh Guards

and has also been awarded to the:-

Royal Tank Regiment
Derbyshire Yeomanry
Lothians and Border Horse
Royal Hampshire Regiment
Rifle Brigade
Tower Hamlets Rifles

PICHON
8th April, 1943

In this subsidiary Action, 128th Brigade Group carried out an attack towards Djebel el Rhorab.

The Honour has been awarded to the:-

Royal Hampshire Regiment

DJEBEL EL RHORAB
9th April, 1943

1st Guards Brigade and 26th Armoured Brigade took part in this subsidiary Action which captured this dominating feature.

The Honour has been awarded to the:-

Welsh Guards

FONDOUK PASS
9th April, 1943

In this subsidiary Action, 26th Armoured Brigade successfully attacked and captured the eastern end of the Pass.

The Honour has been awarded to the:-

Rifle Brigade   Tower Hamlets Rifles

SIDI ALI
10th April, 1943

British armoured units captured the position, with 400 prisoners, in this subsidiary Engagement.

The Honour has been awarded to the:-

Lothians and Border Horse

KAIROUAN
10th April, 1943

In this subsidiary Engagement, 26th Armoured Brigade fought a tank Battle south-west of Kairouan.

The Honour is borne on the Guidon of the:-

Derbyshire Yeomanry

and was also awarded to the:-

16th/5th Lancers

BORDJ
11th April, 1943

An enemy armoured counter-attack was defeated by 26th Armoured Brigade in this subsidiary Engagement.

The Honour is borne on the Guidon of the:-
- 16th/5th Lancers

and has also been awarded to the:-
- Lothians and Border Horse.

OUED ZARGA
7th to 15th April, 1943

This Battle, fought by V Corps, comprised a successful advance to occupy the area Touhabeur-Chaouach and the country to the north including the Beja-Sidi Nair road.

The Honour is borne on the Colours of the:-

East Surrey Regiment	Royal Irish Fusiliers

and has also been awarded to the:-

Lancashire Fusiliers	Northamptonshire Regiment
Royal Inniskilling Fusiliers	Royal West Kent Regiment

MERGUEB CHAOUACH
7th April, 1943

In this subsidiary Action, 36th Brigade captured Djebel el Nahel and Mergueb Chaouach.

The Honour has been awarded to the:-
- North Irish Horse

DJEBEL BEL MAHDI
7th April, 1943

This position was captured, with Djebel M'Kackbia, by 38th Brigade in this subsidiary Action.

The Honour has been awarded to the:-

Royal Inniskilling Fusiliers	Royal Irish Fusiliers

DJEBEL BECH CHEKAOUI
9th April, 1943

In this subsidiary Engagement, Point 667 was captured by 5/Buffs and held against strong counter-attacks.

The Honour has been awarded to the:-
- Buffs

DEJEBEL RMEL
10th April, 1943

To assist the advance of 38th Brigade on Oum Guerinat, N.I.H. seized Djebel Rmel in this subsidiary Engagement.

The Honour is borne on the Guidon of the:-
North Irish Horse

DJEBEL ANG
14th to 15th April, 1943

In this subsidiary Engagement, 11th and 38th Brigades, captured, lost and recaptured this feature.

The Honour has been awarded to the:-

East Surrey Regiment	Royal West Kent Regiment
	Royal Irish Fusiliers

DJEBEL TANNGOUCHA
14th to 25th April, 1943

In this Action, severe fighting took place by 11th and 38th Brigades before this dominating feature was occupied.

The Honour is borne on the Colours of the:-

Royal Inniskilling Fusiliers	Royal Irish Fusiliers

and has also been awarded to the:-
Northamptonshire Regiment

HEIDOUS
15th to 25th April, 1943

In this Engagement, 38th Brigade made repeated attacks before gaining possession of the village.

The Honour has been awarded to the:-

Buffs	London Irish Rifles

BANANA RIDGE
21st April, 1943

3rd Brigade (1st Division) held their positions, in this Action, after heavy fighting.

The Honour has been awarded to the:-

Duke of Wellington's Regiment	The Loyal Regiment

DJEBEL KESSKISS
21st April, 1943

10th Brigade (4th Division) and 2nd Brigade (1st Division) were responsible in this Engagement, for the repulse of enemy attacks on 10th Brigade's position.

The Honour is borne on the Colours of the:- Loyal Regiment

and has also been awarded to the: North Staffordshire Regiment

DJEBEL DJAFFA PASS
21st to 22nd April, 1943

In this Action, the enemy penetrated the front of 10th Brigade, but was eventually thrown back.

The Honour has been awarded to the:- East Surrey Regiment

EL KOURZIA
22nd to 26th April, 1943

In this Battle, fought by IX Corps with 1st Division, 6th Armoured Division, and 46th Division, it was planned to break through the enemy line north of Bou Arada, after which the armour would exploit north-eastwards. The defence was, however, too stubborn. After eight days of heavy fighting the offensive was discontinued.

The Honour is borne on the Guidon of the:-

17th/21st Lancers

and has also been awarded to the:-

Queen's Bays	Derbyshire Yeomanry
9th Lancers	Royal Hampshire Regiment
10th Hussars	Durham Light Infantry
12th Lancers	Rifle Brigade
Royal Tank Regiment	Tower Hamlets Rifles
Yorkshire Dragoons	

BER RABAL
22nd April, 1943

128th Brigade (46th Division), were checked near Mehalla in this subsidiary Action, and driven back.

The Honour has been awarded to the:-

Royal Hampshire Regiment

ARGOUB SELLAH
22nd April, 1943

In this subsidiary Action, 138th Brigade (46th Division) seized the hills, and 26th Armoured Brigade exploited for a further two miles.

The Honour is borne on the Colours of the:-

King's Own Yorkshire Light Infantry

and has also been awarded to the:-

Royal Lincolnshire Regiment

MEDJEZ PLAIN

23rd to 30th April, 1943

This Battle, fought by V Corps with 1st, 4th and 78th Divisions and 25th Tank Brigade, became one with three independent thrusts.

The Honour is borne on the Colours of the:-

    Grenadier Guards   Royal West Kent Regiment
    Duke of Cornwall's Light Infantry   North Staffordshire Regiment

and has also been awarded to the:-

    Royal Tank Regiment   Black Watch
    Scots Guards   Sherwood Foresters
    Irish Guards   Loyal Regiment
    Buffs   Gordon Highlanders
    East Surrey Regiment   Argyll and Sutherland Highlanders
    Duke of Wellington's Regiment

GRICH EL OUED

23rd April, 1943

24th Guards Brigade (1st Division) took park in the capture and exploitation of the feature in this subsidiary Action.

The Honour has been awarded to the:-

    Scots Guards

GUERIAT EL ATACH RIDGE

23rd to 24th April, 1943

2nd and 3rd Brigades (1st Division) were involved in considerable fighting here in this subsidiary Action.

The Honour is borne on the Colours of the:-

    Loyal Regiment

and has also been awarded to the:-

    Duke of Wellington's Regiment   North Staffordshire Regiment
    King's Shropshire Light Infantry

LONGSTOP HILL, 1943

23rd to 26th April

In this subsidiary Action, troops of 78th Division assaulted and captured the whole of this very important feature.

The Honour is emblazoned by the:-

    North Irish Horse   Argyll and Sutherland Highlanders
    East Surrey Regiment

and has also been awarded to the:-

    Buffs   Royal West Kent Regiment

PETER'S CORNER

24th April, 1943

In this subsidiary Action, the advance by 12th Brigade (4th Division) was checked.

The Honour has been awarded to the:-

    Royal Fusiliers

SI MEDIENE

25th to 26th April, 1943

In this subsidiary Engagement, 6/B.W. stormed the feature and held it.

The Honour has been awarded to the:-

    Black Watch

DJEBEL BOU AOUKAZ, 1943, I

27th to 28th April

Heavy fighting in this subsidiary Action, fought by 1st Division, ended with the failure of our assault on the position.

The Honour is borne on the Colours of the:-

    Scots Guards   Irish Guards
                                Duke of Wellington's Regiment

(In the case of the Irish Guards and Duke of Wellington's the Honour is without the 'I' or 'II' (see page 91) since both regiments were at the two actions.)

and has also been awarded to the:-

    Loyal Regiment

SI ABDALLAH

27th to 30th April, 1943

In this subsidiary Action, attempts by 12th Brigade to capture Si Abdallah and Cactus Farm failed with heavy casualties.

The Honour has been awarded to the:-

    Duke of Cornwall's Light Infantry   Royal West Kent Regiment

GAB GAB GAP

29th to 30th April, 1943

In this subsidiary Engagement, strong enemy counter-attacks were repelled by 1st Division.

The Honour has been awarded to the:-

    Loyal Regiment   North Staffordshire Regiment

SIDI AHMED

28th to 30th April, 1943

In this subsidiary Engagement, 36th Brigade were unsuccessfully engaged.

The Honour has been awarded to the:-

    Northamptonshire Regiment

DJEBEL KOURNINE

25th to 30th April, 1943

In this Engagement, 26th Armoured and 1st Guards Brigades (both of 6th Armoured Division), 138th Brigade (46th Division), and 7th Motor Brigade (1st Armoured Division), were involved in five unsuccessful attempts to capture this feature.

The Honour is borne on the Guidon of the:-

    16th/5th Lancers

and has also been awarded to the:-

Queen's Bays	Lothians and Border Horse
10th Hussars	York and Lancaster Regiment
12th Lancers	Rifle Brigade

ARGOUB EL MEGAS

30th April, 1943

1/K.R.R.C. captured this feature in this Engagement.

The Honour has been awarded to the:-

    King's Royal Rifle Corps

TUNIS

5th to 12th May, 1943

The last Battle in North Africa, leading to the capture of the Tunisian Bridgehead and the liquidation of the enemy forces in North Africa, was fought by First Army with V and IX Corps and U.S. forces, and included units passed from Eighth to First Army. 1st, 6th and 7th Armoured Divisions, 25th Tank Brigade, 3rd, 4th, 78th and 4th Indian Divisions, took part.

The Honour is emblazoned by the:-

King's Dragoon Guards	North Irish Horse
Queen's Bays	Honourable Artillery Company
10th Hussars	Coldstream Guards
11th Hussars	Bedfordshire and Hertfordshire Regiment
12th Lancers	Black Watch
16th/5th Lancers	Sherwood Foresters
17/21st Lancers	King's Shropshire Light Infantry
Yorkshire Dragoons	2nd Gurkha Rifles
Derbyshire Yeomanry	Tower Hamlets Rifles
3rd/4th County of London Yeomanry	

and has also been awarded to the:-

9th Lancers	Essex Regiment
Royal Tank Regiment	Royal West Kent Regiment
Lothians and Border Horse	King's Royal Rifle Corps
Welsh Guards	Rifle Brigade
Queen's Royal Regiment	London Rifle Brigade
East Surrey Regiment	Royal Sussex Regiment
Duke of Wellington's Regiment	

DJEBEL BOU AOUKAZ, 1943, II

5th to 6th May

3rd Brigade captured and held this feature, in this subsidiary Action, prior to the launching of the main attack by IX Corps.

The Honour has been awarded to the:-

King's Shropshire Light Infantry

Note: See *DJEBEL BOU AOUKAZ, 1943, I* - page 89 - for Irish Guards and Duke of Wellington's.

MONTARNAUD

6th May, 1943

In this subsidiary Action, the objective was captured by 10th Brigade, and exploited by 12th Brigade.

The Honour has been awarded to the:-

East Surrey Regiment

RAGOUBET SOUISSI

6th May

4th Indian Division, with 25th Tank Brigade, had two brigades involved in the fighting on this feature.

The Honour has been awarded to the:-

Essex Regiment

HAMMAM LIF

8th to 9th May, 1943

In this subsidiary Action, 26th Armoured and 1st Guards Brigades, after being initially held up, broke through and overcame enemy resistance. 2/Lothians supported by 17/21 L. moved along the beach.

The Honour is emblazoned by the:-

Lothians and Border Horse	Welsh Guards

and has also been awarded to the:-

17th/21st Lancers	Rifle Brigade
Coldstream Guards	Tower Hamlets Rifles

CRETEVILLE PASS

8th to 11th May, 1943

1/Derby Yeo. were held up on the 8th by anti-tank guns and tanks at the entrance to the Pass. 2nd Armoured and 7th Motor Brigade then fought, in this subsidiary Engagement, throughout 10th May in the Pass, which was finally forced in the early hours of the 11th.

The Honour has been awarded to the:-

Queen's Bays	12th Lancers
9th Lancers	

GROMBALLA

10th May, 1943

In this subsidiary Engagement, 26th Armoured Brigade were held up when approaching Gromballa from the north. An entry was forced, and some two battalions of Italian infantry surrendered.

The Honour was awarded to the:-

16th/5th Lancers

BOU FICHA

11th May, 1943

This subsidiary Engagement marked the close of the Tunisian campaign. 26th Armoured Brigade broke through a minefield covered by anti-tank guns along the Wadi Cherchar to capture the town.

The Honour has been awarded to the:-

16th/5th Lancers	Lothians and Border Horse

SICILY, 1943

The campaign lasted from 9th July to 17th August, 1943. The capture of the island had five important results: it made the Mediterranean sea route more secure, established a base for the further attack on Italy (especially air attack), diverted some German strength from the Russian front during the summer period, precipitated the collapse of Italy, and dealt the enemy a heavy blow to his prestige.

The forces included the British Eighth Army and the American Seventh Army. The Eighth Army, under General Montgomery, included XIII Corps (5th and 50th Divisions, elements of 1st Airborne Division, and 4th Armoured Brigade) and XXX Corps (51st, 78th and 1st Canadian Divisions, 23rd Armoured and 231st Infantry Brigades).

The Theatre Honour of 'Sicily, 1943' was emblazoned by the:-

Royal Dragoons
Royal Tank Regiment
3rd/4th County of London Yeomanry
Honourable Artillery Company
Buffs
East Yorkshire Regiment
Green Howards
Cheshire Regiment
Cameronians
Royal Inniskilling Fusiliers

East Surrey Regiment
South Staffordshire Regiment
Black Watch
Royal Berkshire Regiment
King's Own Yorkshire Light Infantry
Middlesex Regiment
York & Lancaster Regiment
Seaforth Highlanders
Glider Pilot Regiment
London Irish Rifles

and has also been awarded to the:-

Devonshire Regiment
Lancashire Fusiliers
Royal Scots Fusiliers
Royal Hampshire Regiment
Dorset Regiment
Welch Regiment
Northamptonshire Regiment
Royal West Kent Regiment
Wiltshire Regiment

Durham Light Infantry
Highland Light Infantry
Gordon Highlanders
Cameron Highlanders
Argyll and Sutherland Highlanders
Parachute Regiment
London Scottish
Special Air Service Regiment
Kensington Regiment
Commando Association

LANDING IN SICILY

9th to 12th July, 1943

This Battle, which included the airborne drop, covered the successful initial assault by Eighth Army in the south-eastern quarter of the island.

The Honour was emblazoned by the:-

Devonshire Regiment
Royal Scots Fusiliers
Border Regiment
Dorset Regiment

South Staffordshire Regiment
Highland Light Infantry
Glider Pilot Regiment
Special Air Service Regiment

and has also been awarded to the:-

3rd/4th County of London Yeomanry   Black Watch

Green Howards	Northamptonshire Regiment
Cheshire Regiment	Durham Light Infantry
Cameronians	Seaforth Highlanders
Royal Inniskilling Fusiliers	Gordon Highlanders
Royal Hampshire Regiment	Argyll and Sutherland Highlanders
York & Lancaster Regiment	Commando Association

SOLARINO

11th to 13th July, 1943

In this Engagement, the advance of 13th Brigade was heavily opposed by infantry, artillery and dive bombers, but it succeeded in cutting the lateral road and protecting the left flank of 5th Division's advance on Augusta.

The Honour has been awarded to the:-

Royal Inniskilling Fusiliers	Durham Light Infantry
Wiltshire Regiment	

VIZZINI

11th to 14th July, 1943

23rd Armoured Brigade, 231st Brigade, and 153rd and 154th Brigades of 51st Division, were all involved in severe fighting before compelling the enemy to withdraw.

The Honour has been awarded to the:-

Black Watch

AUGUSTA

12th to 13th July, 1943

17th Brigade, with 4th Armoured Brigade, overcame strong points in this Engagement.

The Honour has been awarded to the:-

Seaforth Highlanders

FRANCOFONTE

13th to 15th July, 1943

In this Engagement, 152nd Brigade captured Francofonte.

The Honour has been awarded to the:-

Middlesex Regiment	Cameron Highlanders
Seaforth Highlanders	

LENTINI and PRIMOSOLE BRIDGE

13th to 18th July, 1943

In this Action, 1st Parachute Brigade, 151st Brigade, and 4th Armoured Brigade, with 3 Commando, captured the bridge after strong opposition and formed a bridgehead. This was an essential part of the plan to capture Catania.

'Primosole Bridge' is borne on the Colours of the:-

    Durham Light Infantry   London Scottish
    Parachute Regiment

and has also been awarded to the:-

    Royal Tank Regiment   Cheshire Regiment
    East Yorkshire Regiment

'Lentini' has been awarded to the:-

    3rd/4th County of London Yeomanry   London Irish Rifles
    Green Howards

SFERRO

15th to 20th July, 1943

153rd Brigade, with some help from 23rd Armoured Brigade, captured the town in this Engagement.

The Honour is borne on the Colours of the:-   Gordon Highlanders

and has also been awarded to the:-

    Black Watch   Middlesex Regiment

SIMETO BRIDGEHEAD

18th to 21st July, 1943

13th Brigade was concerned with this Engagement.

The Honour has been awarded to the:-

    3rd/4th County of London Yeomanry   Royal Inniskilling Fusiliers
    Cheshire Regiment   Wiltshire Regiment
    Cameronians   York & Lancashire Regiment
          London Irish Rifles

GERBINI

18th to 21st July, 1943

154th Brigade, with the help of 23rd Armoured Brigade, were involved in the fighting in this Engagement.

The Honour has been awarded to the:-

    Royal Tank Regiment   Argyll and Sutherland Highlanders
    Black Watch

AGIRA

24th to 28th July, 1943

In this Action, 1st and 2nd Canadian Brigades met with varying success, while 231st Infantry Brigade, having successfully attacked, was forced to withdraw five times to conform to the Canadians.

The Honour has been awarded to the:-

    Dorset Regiment

ADRANO

29th July to 7th August, 1943

This Battle, successfully fought by XXX Corps, consisted of a series of Actions and Engagements, culminating with the fall of Adrano which broke the 'Etna line.'

1st Canadian, 50th and 78th Divisions, 23rd Armoured and 231st Infantry Brigades, took part.

The Honour has been awarded to the:-

Royal Tank Regiment	Seaforth Highlanders
Lancashire Fusiliers	Cameron Highlanders
Royal Inniskilling Fusiliers	Royal Irish Fusiliers
East Surrey Regiment	Argyll and Sutherland Highlanders
Black Watch	London Irish Rifles
Northamptonshire Regiment	

REGALBUTO

29th July to 3rd August, 1943

231st and 1st Canadian Brigades succeeded in capturing Regalbuto, in this subsidiary Engagement, in face of heavy opposition, and thus opened the road to Adrano.

The Honour is borne on the Colours of the:-

Devonshire Regiment

and has also been awarded to the:-

Royal Hampshire Regiment   Dorset Regiment

SFERRO HILLS

31st July to 3rd August, 1943

This successful subsidiary Action was fought by 51st Division and 23rd Armoured Brigade. Heavy fighting took place, particularly by 152nd Brigade.

The Honour has been awarded to the:-

Black Watch	Seaforth Highlanders
Middlesex Regiment	Cameron Highlanders

CENTURIPE

31st July to 3rd August, 1943

In this subsidiary Action, 11th Brigade (78th Division) successfully enlarged the Catanuova Bridgehead, while Centuripe was first unsuccessfully and then successfully attacked by 36th and 38th Brigades respectively.

The Honour was emblazoned by the:-

Royal Inniskilling Fusiliers	Kensington Regiment
Royal West Kent Regiment	Royal Irish Fusiliers

and has also been awarded to the:-

Buffs	Argyll and Sutherland Highlanders
East Surrey Regiment	London Irish Rifles

SALSO CROSSING

4th August, 1943

38th Brigade overcame stubborn resistance in this subsidiary Engagement, exploiting forward some 2,000 yards.

The Honour has been awarded to the:-

    Royal Irish Fusiliers   London Irish Rifles

SIMETO CROSSING

5th August, 1943

This subsidiary Engagement was fiercely contested by 38th Brigade successfully established a bridgehead, thereby opening the way for the direct attack on the key town of Adrano.

The Honour has been awarded to the:-

    Royal Inniskilling Fusiliers   London Irish Rifles
    Royal Irish Fusiliers

MONTE RIVOGLIA

9th August, 1943

36th Brigade, with some assistance from 23rd Armoured Brigade, captured the objective in face of heavy opposition in this Engagement, thereby opening the road to Malleto.

The Honour has been awarded to the:-

    Buffs   Royal West Kent Regiment

MALLETO

12th to 13th August, 1943.

This Engagement was a successful operation, leading to the fall of Randazzo, fought by 38th Infantry and 23rd Armoured Brigades.

The Honour has been awarded to the:-

    Royal Irish Fusiliers   London Irish Rifles

PURSUIT TO MESSINA

2nd to 17th August, 1943

This was the last Action of the Sicilian Campaign, in which 5th, 50th and 51st Divisions, with 4th Armoured Brigade, participated.

During this Action, enemy rearguards were destroyed, Catania was captured, and an amphibious operation carried out.

The Honour has been awarded to the:-

    Royal Inniskilling Fusiliers   London Irish Rifles
    Royal Berkshire Regiment   Commando Association
    York and Lancaster Regiment

ITALY, 1943 – 45

The campaign in Italy was remarkable for its contrasts in climate and terrain. It suffered to some extent from changing policies which, by withdrawing formations for employment elsewhere, precluded the commanders of the remaining Allied forces from achieving considerable successes which would otherwise have been within their grasp. Nevertheless, a great measure of success was achieved, and the German Armies in Italy were the first to surrender in Europe.

More than thirty regiments were represented in the theatre throughout the campaign.

The Honour 'Italy, 1943-45' is borne on the Colours of the:-

Royal Tank Regiment
Coldstream Guards
Scots Guards
Royal Leicestershire Regiment
Royal Inniskilling Fusiliers
East Surrey Regiment
Welch Regiment
Northamptonshire Regiment
King's Shropshire Light Infantry
King's Royal Rifle Corps
Argyll and Sutherland Highlanders
Rifle Brigade
London Irish Rifles
Special Air Service Regiment

and has also been awarded to the:-

Grenadier Guards
Queen's Royal Regiment
Buffs
Royal Northumberland Fusiliers
Royal Fusiliers
Royal Lincolnshire Regiment
Lancashire Fusiliers
Cheshire Regiment
Duke of Wellington's Regiment
Royal Hampshire Regiment
Oxfordshire and Buckinghamshire Light Infantry
Sherwood Foresters
Royal Berkshire Regiment
Royal West Kent Regiment
King's Own Yorkshire Light Infantry
York and Lancaster Regiment
Durham Light Infantry
London Scottish
Kensington Regiment
Commando Association

The Honour 'Italy, 1943' is borne on the Guidons of the:-

Royal Dragoons
11th Hussars
3rd/4th County of London Yeomanry

and has also been awarded to the:-

Royal Scots Greys
Devonshire Regiment
South Staffordshire Regiment
Dorset Regiment

The Honour 'Italy, 1943, '45,' has been awarded to the:-

Highland Light Infantry

The Honour 'Italy, 1943-44,' is borne on the Standard and Appointments of the:-

King's Dragoon Guards
Cameronians
Queen's Westminsters

and has also been awarded to the:-

    Irish Guards
    Green Howards
    Royal Scots Fusiliers
    Essex Regiment
    Wiltshire Regiment
    Seaforth Highlanders
    Parachute Regiment

The Honour 'Italy, 1944' is borne on the Standards and Guidons of the:-

    Life Guards
    Royal Horse Guards
    3rd Hussars
    Warwickshire Yeomanry
    Yorkshire Dragoons

and has also been awarded to the:-

    Royal Wiltshire Yeomanry
    Manchester Regiment
    Cameron Highlanders
    7th Gurkha Rifles

The Honour 'Italy, 1944-45' has been emblazoned by the:-

    7th Hussars
    9th Lancers
    12th Lancers
    16th/5th Lancers
    17th/21st Lancers
    27th Lancers
    Lothians and Border Horse
    North Irish Horse
    Royal Scots
    Somerset Light Infantry
    Bedfordshire and Hertfordshire Regiment
    Royal Sussex Regiment
    Loyal Regiment
    6th Gurkha Rifles
    Hertfordshire Regiment
    London Rifle Brigade
    Tower Hamlets Rifles

and has also been awarded to the:-

    Queen's Bays
    4th Hussars
    10th Hussars
    Derbyshire Yeomanry
    Honourable Artillery Company
    Welsh Guards
    King's Own Royal Regiment
    King's Regiment
    Duke of Cornwall's Light Infantry
    Black Watch
    Middlesex Regiment
    North Staffordshire Regiment
    Gordon Highlanders
    2nd Gurkha Rifles
    10th Gurkha Rifles

The Honour 'Italy, 1945' is borne on the Guidon of the:-

    14th/20th Hussars

LANDING AT PORTO SAN VENERE

8th September, 1943

In this Action, 231st Brigade Group successfully secured a beach-head, meeting some strong opposition and counter-attacks.

The Honour has been awarded to the:-

    Devonshire Regiment
    Dorset Regiment
    Royal Hampshire Regiment
    Commando Association

TARANTO

9th to 22nd September, 1943

1st Airborne Division successfully established a bridgehead for the protection of Taranto in this Action.

The Honour has been awarded to the:-

    Parachute Regiment

TERMOLI

3rd to 6th October, 1943

In this Action, 78th Division advanced on Termoli overland, while the Special Service (S.S.) Brigade seized Termoli from the sea on 3rd October. Between 4th and 6th October, heavy counter-attacks were made on the bridgehead by German paratroops, and losses on both sides were heavy.

The Honour was emblazoned by the:-

Royal Irish Fusiliers	Special Air Service Regiment
Kensington Regiment	

and has also been awarded to the:-

3rd/4th County of London Yeomanry	Royal West Kent Regiment
Buffs	Argyll and Sutherland Highlanders
Lancashire Fusiliers	London Irish Rifles
Royal Inniskilling Fusiliers	Commando Association

TRIGNO

22nd October to 5th November, 1943

This Action was fought by V Corps. 78th and 8th Indian Divisions each established a bridgehead after hard fighting.

The Honour was emblazoned by the:-

    Buffs

and was also awarded to the:-

Lancashire Fusiliers	Essex Regiment
Royal Inniskilling Fusiliers	Royal Irish Fusiliers
East Surrey Regiment	London Irish Rifles

SAN SALVO

2nd to 3rd November, 1943

The capture of this position led to the collapse of the enemy on the Trigno. 36th Brigade fought this Engagement, with supporting arms.

The Honour has been awarded to the:-

Royal Inniskilling Fusiliers	Royal West Kent Regiment

SANGRO

19th November to 3rd December, 1943

This Battle, fought by Eighth Army, precipitated the enemy withdrawal and destroyed a valuable defensive outpost of the winter line. V Corps (78th, 2nd New Zealand, and 8th Indian Divisions, with 4th Armoured Brigade) took part, with diversionary operations by 1st Canadian Division and 5th Division of XIII Corps.

The Honour is borne on the Colours of the:-

    3rd/4th County of London Yeomanry   Royal West Kent Regiment
    Lancashire Fusiliers   Royal Irish Fusiliers
    East Surrey Regiment   London Irish Rifles
    Essex Regiment   Kensington Regiment

and has also been awarded to the:-

    Royal Tank Regiment   Northamptonshire Regiment
    Buffs   King's Royal Rifle Corps
    Royal Fusiliers   Argyll and Sutherland Highlanders
    Royal Scots Fusiliers
    Cheshire Regiment
    Royal Inniskilling Fusiliers

MOZZAGROGNA

27th to 29th November, 1943

In this subsidiary Action, 17th Indian Brigade (1/R.F., 1/5 R. Gurkha Rif., 1/12 Frontier Force Regt., supported by 50/R.T.R) twice captured the town, being forced out after the first attack.

The Honour is borne on the Colours of the:-

    Royal Fusiliers

FOSSACESIA

30th November, 1943

38th Irish Brigade, and 4th Armoured Brigade, successfully attacked in this subsidiary Action, which opened the way for the advance to the Moro.

The Honour has been awarded to the:-

    3rd/4th County of London Yeomanry   London Irish Rifles
    Royal Irish Fusiliers

ROMAGNOLI

30th November to 1st December, 1943

Romagnoli was a German strongpoint between Mozzagrogna and Lanciano. A sharp attack by 5/R.W.K., in 21st Indian Brigade, followed by the defeat of a German counter-attack, marked this Engagement.

The Honour has been awarded to the:-

    Royal West Kent Regiment

ORSOGNA

3rd to 24th December, 1943

2nd New Zealand Division, 2nd Independent Parachute Brigade, and 17th Brigade (5th Division) took part in this Action, which included four attacks against determined opposition, accompanied by bitter fighting.

The Honour has been awarded to the:-

Parachute Regiment

IMPOSSIBLE BRIDGE

5th to 13th December, 1943

In this Engagement, the bridgehead was seized and held to enable a bridge to be built over the River Moro. It was held against severe counter-attacks. The units involved were 5/R.W.K., 3/15 Punjab Regt., 1/5 Mahrattas, and 50/R.T.R., all under command of 21st Indian Brigade in 8th Indian Div.

The Honour has been awarded to the:-

Royal West Kent Regiment

CALDARI

13th to 14th December, 1943

In this Engagement, 1/R.F., in 17th Indian Brigade, took part in an attack which captured Caldari and held it against counter-attacks, thereby securing positions over the River Moro.

The Honour has been awarded to the:-

Royal Fusiliers

VILLA GRANDE

22nd to 28th December, 1943

19th and 21st Indian Infantry Brigades of the 8th Indian Division were involved in this Action. 5 Essex with a company each of 3/8 Punjab and 6/13 Frontier Force Rifles in the 19th Brigade, and 5 R.W.K., with 3/15 Punjab, 1/5 Mahrattas 6th Lancers and 50 R.T.R. under command of 21st Brigade, took part in the operation in which there was heavy fighting. It assisted 1st Canadian Division in its attack on Ortona.

The Honour was emblazoned by the:-

Essex Regiment

and was also awarded to the:-

Royal West Kent Regiment

SALERNO

9th to 18th September, 1943

This Battle was fought by Fifth U.S. Army, having under command 7th Armoured Division, 23rd Armoured and the 2nd S.S. Brigades). A bridgehead was established in the face of heavy and constant counter attacks in which seven German divisions were involved. The capture of Naples followed on this operation, in which some 5,000 British casualties were sustained.

The Honour is borne on the Guidon and Colours of the:-

Royal Scots Greys	Cheshire Regiment
Grenadier Guards	Royal Hampshire Regiment
Coldstream Guards	Oxfordshire and Buckinghamshire Light Infantry
Queen's Royal Regiment	Sherwood Foresters
Royal Northumberland Fusiliers	King's Own Yorkshire Light Infantry
Royal Fusiliers	York and Lancaster Regiment
Royal Lincolnshire Regiment	Durham Light Infantry
Royal Leicestershire Regiment	

and has also been awarded to the:-

Royal Tank Regiment Commando Association
Scots Guards

SANTA LUCIA

9th to 16th September, 1943

In this subsidiary Action, 167th Brigade and 23rd Armoured Brigade captured and held this position, vital to the flank of X Corps.

The Honour has been awarded to the:-

Royal Fusiliers Oxfordshire and Buckinghamshire Light Infantry
Cheshire Regiment

VIETRI PASS

9th to 16th September, 1943

This area was captured, in this subsidiary Action, by the S.S. Brigade (2 and 41 (R.M.) Commandos) and held against strong counter-attacks, in which 138th Brigade were involved.

The Honour has been awarded to the:-

Royal Lincolnshire Regiment York and Lancaster Regiment

SALERNO HILLS

9th to 17th September, 1943

46th Division, with the S.S. Brigade and 167th Brigade of 56th Division, captured and held the high ground overlooking the Salerno beach, in this subsidiary Action.

The Honour has been awarded to the:-

Royal Hampshire Regiment King's Own Yorkshire Light Infantry
Oxfordshire and Buckinghamshire Light Infantry

BATTIPAGLIA

10th to 18th September, 1943

The Battipaglia 'Tobacco Factory' positions were vital to the enemy and to Fifth Army. They were captured on the 10th September, in this subsidiary Action, but recaptured by the Germans after severe fighting. After close and continuous fighting, the areas were finally captured on the 18th September. 56th Division, with

23rd Armoured Brigade, and 131st Lorried Infantry Brigade of 7th Armoured Division, were involved.

The Honour has been awarded to the:-

> Royal Scots Greys
> Coldstream Guards
> Scots Guards
> Royal Fusiliers
> Cheshire Regiment
> Royal Hampshire Regiment

CAPTURE OF NAPLES

22nd September to 1st October, 1943

This Battle began with the break-out against heavy opposition of 46th Division though the Salerno hills, thus opening the route to Naples, which 7th Armoured Division secured after some sharp fighting. 56th Division protected the flank and pressed the enemy.

The Honour has been awarded to the:-

> King's Dragoons Guards
> 11th Hussars
> Royal Lincolnshire Regiment
> York and Lancaster Regiment

CAVA DI TIRRENI

22nd to 28th September, 1943

This subsidiary Action by 46th Division, enabled the armour to break out of the mountains and advance on Naples.

The Honour has been awarded to the:-

> Royal Lincolnshire Regiment
> Royal Hampshire Regiment
> King's Own Yorkshire Light Infantry
> York and Lancaster Regiment

CAPPEZANO

24th to 25th September, 1943

In this subsidiary Engagement, 201st Guards Bde. (56th Division) captured a strong position after heavy fighting, to enable the division to advance.

The Honour has been awarded to the:-

> Coldstream Guards

MONTE STELLA

24th to 26th September, 1943

This feature was captured by 169th Brigade, after two attacks, in this subsidiary Engagement.

The Honour has been awarded to the:-

> Queen's Royal Regiment

SCAFATI BRIDGE

28th September, 1943

This was an important bridge on the main Salerno-Naples road, and the enemy was preparing its demolition when it was captured. Heavy counter-attacks by infantry and armour were then defeated, in this subsidiary Engagement.

The Honour has been awarded to the:-

King's Dragoon Guards   Queen's Royal Regiment

CARDITO

3rd October, 1943

In this Engagement, 22nd Armoured Brigade overcame a strong enemy position which was holding up the advance of 7th Armoured Division.

The Honour has been awarded to the:-

Rifle Brigade

VOLTURNO CROSSING

12th to 25th October, 1943

In this Battle, fought by VI U.S. Corps and X Corps under command of Fifth U.S. Army, five German divisions opposed six Allied divisions. The first crossings were only partially successful, but after heavy fighting the enemy was forced to withdraw, thus opening the way for the attack on the 'Winter Line.'

The Honour has been awarded to the:-

Royal Scots Greys   Royal Lincolnshire Regiment
11th Hussars   Cheshire Regiment
Royal Tank Regiment   Royal Hampshire Regiment
3rd/4th County of London Yeomanry   Sherwood Foresters
Grenadier Guards   King's Own Yorkshire Light Infantry
Coldstream Guards   York and Lancaster Regiment
Scots Guards   Durham Light Infantry
Queen's Royal Regiment
Royal Northumberland Fusiliers

MONTE MARO

22nd to 23rd October, 1943

This subsidiary Engagement, in which 169th Brigade were supported by the machine-guns of the 6/Cheshire, captured dominating features on Route 7 to enable 56th Division to advance.

The Honour has been awarded to the:-

Cheshire Regiment

ROCCHETTA E CROCE
22nd to 23rd October, 1943

This subsidiary Engagement involved 201st Guards Brigade in the capture of dominating high ground on the line of advance.

The Honour has been awarded to the:-

    Scots Guards

TEANO
28th to 31st October, 1943

The capture, in this Action, of the important communication centre of Teano by 56th Division led to a deep enemy withdrawal.

The Honour is borne on the Colours of the:-

    London Scottish

and has also been awarded to the:-

Royal Fusiliers	Durham Light Infantry
Cheshire Regiment	London Irish Rifles
Oxfordshire and Buckinghamshire Light Infantry	

MONTE CAMINO
5th November to 9th December, 1943

A hard and sustained struggle for this great mountain mass, which was an important outpost of the 'Winter Line,' constituted this Battle, in which the advantages of the ground lay with the enemy. X Corps fought under command of Fifth U.S. Army.

The Honour is borne on the Colours of the:-

King's Dragoon Guards	Queen's Royal Regiment
Grenadier Guards	London Scottish
Scots Guards	

and has also been awarded to the:-

Coldstream Guards	Sherwood Foresters
Royal Northumberland Fusiliers	Royal Berkshire Regiment
Royal Fusiliers	York and Lancaster Regiment
Cheshire Regiment	Durham Light Infantry
Oxfordshire and Buckinghamshire Light Infantry	London Irish Rifles

CALABRITTO
5th November to 6th December, 1943

In this subsidiary Action, 201st Guards, 168th and 139th Brigades were successively involved in severe fighting in this area.

The Honour has been awarded to the:-

Coldstream Guards	York and Lancaster Regiment

Royal Leicestershire Regiment
Royal Berkshire Regiment
London Scottish
London Irish Rifles

COLLE CEDRO

4th to 9th January, 1944

This Action, resulting in the capture of the area after stubborn fighting involving 138th and 139th Brigades, enabled Fifth Army to advance towards Cassino.

The Honour has been awarded to the:-

York and Lancaster Regiment

GARIGLIANO CROSSING

17th to 31st January, 1944

In this Battle, X Corps established a bridgehead against heavy opposition, but failed to advance from it. The Corps sustained over 4,000 casualties.

The Honour is borne on the Colours and Appointments of the:-

Royal Fusiliers
Royal Scots Fusiliers
Royal Inniskilling Fusiliers
Northamptonshire Regiment

Wiltshire Regiment
London Scottish
London Irish Rifles

and has also been awarded to the:-

King's Dragoons Guards
Royal Tank Regiment
Coldstream Guards
Queen's Royal Regiment
Royal Northumberland Fusiliers
Royal Lincolnshire Regiment
Cheshire Regiment
Cameronians
Royal Hampshire Regiment

Oxfordshire and Buckinghamshire Light Infantry
Royal Berkshire Regiment
King's Own Yorkshire Light Infantry
York and Lancaster Regiment
Seaforth Highlanders

MINTURNO

17th to 25th January, 1944

In this subsidiary Action, 5th Division met with strong opposition establishing a bridgehead over the Garigliano and capturing Minturno.

The Honour is borne on the Colours of the:-

Green Howards
King's Own Yorkshire Light Infantry

York and Lancaster Regiment

and has also been awarded to the:-

Royal Scots Fusiliers
Cheshire Regiment
Royal Inniskilling Fusiliers

Wiltshire Regiment

DAMIANO

18th to 30th January, 1944

In this subsidiary Action, 56th Division (with 128th Brigade of 46th Division, and 40 (R.M) Commando), continuously attacked with varying success, while counter-attacks were at the same time being defeated.

The Honour is emblazoned by the:-

    Royal Berkshire Regiment

and has also been awarded to the:-

Queen's Royal Regiment	Oxfordshire and Buckinghamshire Light Infantry
Royal Fusiliers	London Scottish
Cheshire Regiment	London Irish Rifles
Royal Hampshire Regiment	

MONTE TUGA

26th to 30th January, 1944

In this subsidiary Action, 138th Brigade, with 2/5 Foresters and 16/D.L.I. of 139th Brigade, captured a series of heights of which Monte Tuga was one, thus providing a firm base for further advances.

The Honour has been awarded to the:-

Royal Lincolnshire Regiment	York and Lancaster Regiment
King's Own Yorkshire Light Infantry	Durham Light Infantry

MONTE ORNITO

2nd to 20th February, 1944

In this hard-fought Action, 2nd S.S. Brigade attacked on 2nd February, and captured Monte Ornito. 5/Hampshires and 1st Guards Brigade both subsequently occupied and held this important position against heavy and sustained counter-attacks. Over 750 British casualties were suffered.

The Honour is borne on the Colours of the:-

Coldstream Guards	Welsh Guards

and has also been awarded to the:-

Royal Hampshire Regiment	Commando Association

CERASOLA

7th to 9th February, 1944

This Engagement was the scene of heavy fighting by 138th Brigade in this mountainous country west of the Garigliano.

The Honour has been awarded to the:-

    Royal Hampshire Regiment

ANZIO

22nd January to 22nd May, 1944

In this Battle, under the command of VI U.S. Corps, 1st, 56th and 5th Divisions, with 2nd S.S. 18th and 24th Guards Brigades, took part in the assault landing, establishment, and holding of the Anzio Bridgehead. Had all gone well initially, the German forces facing the main Allied armies to the south would have been trapped. The fighting was severe, and casualties heavy.

The Honour is borne on the Colours and Appointments of the:-

Yorkshire Dragoons	Loyal Regiment
Grenadier Guards	Northamptonshire Regiment
Scots Guards	Royal Berkshire Regiment
Irish Guards	King's Own Yorkshire Light Infantry
Queen's Royal Regiment	King's Shropshire Light Infantry
Buffs	Middlesex Regiment
Royal Fusiliers	Wiltshire Regiment
Green Howards	North Staffordshire Regiment
Cameronians	Seaforth Highlanders
Duke of Wellington's Regiment	Gordon Highlanders
Oxfordshire and Buckinghamshire Light Infantry	London Scottish
Sherwood Foresters	London Irish Rifles

and has also been awarded to the:-

Royal Tank Regiment	York and Lancaster Regiment
Royal Scots Fusiliers	Commando Association
Cheshire Regiment	
Royal Inniskilling Fusiliers	

APRILIA

24th to 26th January, 1944

In this subsidiary Engagement, in which 24th Guards Brigade took part, the objective which included the 'Tobacco Factory' was captured after heavy fighting and held against counter-attacks by enemy tanks and infantry.

The Honour has been awarded to the:-

Irish Guards

CAMPOLEONE

24th to 31st January, 1944

1st Division, with 24th Guards and 3rd Brigade, and 46/R.T.R., extended the western flank of the bridgehead in this subsidiary action.

The Honour was emblazoned by the:-

Sherwood Foresters

and was also awarded to the:-

Scots Guards	King's Shropshire Light Infantry
Duke of Wellington's Regiment	

CARROCETO

7th to 10th February, 1944

This subsidiary action included the fiercest fighting during the Battle of Anzio. More than twenty-one German infantry battalions attempted to break through, but completely failed to do so. There were heavy losses on both sides. Our own troops were 24th Guards, 2nd, 3rd and 168th Brigade, with 46/R.T.R.

The Honour has been awarded to the:-

Scots Guards	North Staffordshire Regiment
Irish Guards	London Scottish
Royal Berkshire Regiment	London Irish Rifles
King's Shropshire Light Infantry	
Middlesex Regiment	

CASSINO I

20th January to 25th March, 1944

II U.S. Corps and the New Zealand Corps, (with 2nd New Zealand Division, 4th Indian Division and elements of 78th Division) were involved in this Battle. Despite fierce fighting only local gains were made.

The Honour was emblazoned by the:-

East Surrey Regiment*	Royal West Kent Regiment*
Royal Sussex Regiment	2nd Gurkha Rifles
Essex Regiment	7th Gurkha Rifles

and was also awarded to the:-

Buffs	Cameron Highlanders

MONASTERY HILL

15th January to 18th February, 1944

In this subsidiary action, 7th Indian Brigade (1/R.Sussex, 4/16 Punjab, 1/2 Gurkha Rifles), carried out an attack over most difficult ground against the most vital part of the Cassino position. But the main position could not be carried, and the attack failed after heavy fighting.

The Honour has been awarded to the:-

Royal Sussex Regiment	2nd Gurkha Rifles

CASTLE HILL

15th to 24th March, 1944

This subsidiary action began with the capture of the feature by 25th N.Z. Battalion. 5th Indian Brigade (1/4 Essex, 1/6 Rajputana Rifles, 4/6 Rajputana Rifles), and 6/R.W.K. from 78th Division thereafter held the position and repulsed many counter-attacks.

The Honour has been awarded to the:-

Essex Regiment	Royal West Kent Regiment

* Awarded both 'Cassino I' and 'Cassino II' the combined Honour being shown simply as 'Cassino' in the case of these two regiments only.

HANGMAN'S HILL

15th to 25th March, 1944

In this subsidiary action, 5th Indian Brigade held the hill for eight days against heavy enemy counter-attacks, and endured severe losses.

The Honour has been awarded to the:-
    Essex Regiment

CASSINO II

11th to 18th May, 1944

Eighth Army fought this Battle with XIII Corps (4th, 78th and 8th Indian Divisions, 26th and 1st Canadian Armoured Brigades), 1st Canadian Division, and Polish Corps, while X Corps (2nd N.Z. Division, 24th Guards Brigade, 12th South African Motor Brigade, and 'Hermon Force'), carried out diversionary measures on the right flank.

The Honour was emblazoned by the:-

16th/5th Lancers	Royal Inniskilling Fusiliers
17th/21st Lancers	East Surrey Regiment*
Derbyshire Yeomanry	Duke of Cornwall's Light Infantry
Lothians and Border Horse	Royal Hampshire Regiment
Honourable Artillery Company	Black Watch
Royal Northumberland Fusiliers	Northamptonshire Regiment
Royal Fusiliers	Royal West Kent Regiment*
King's Regiment	Royal Irish Fusiliers
Somerset Light Infantry	Rifle Brigade
Bedfordshire and Hertfordshire Regiment	London Irish Rifles
Lancashire Fusiliers	Tower Hamlets Rifles
Kensington Regiment	

and has also been awarded to the:-
    Argyll and Sutherland Highlanders

MASSA VERTECCHI

14th May, 1944

2/4 Hampshire In 28th Brigade, fought this subsidiary Engagement, capturing this important strongpoint in face of heavy opposition, and by hand-to-hand fighting.

The Honour has been awarded to the:-
    Royal Hampshire Regiment

MASSA TAMBOURINI

15th May, 1944

In this subsidiary engagement, 6/Innisks (38th Brigade) captured this strongpoint after hard fighting.

The Honour has been awarded to the:-   Royal Inniskilling Fusiliers

---

* Awarded both 'Cassino I' and 'Cassino II' the combined Honour being shown simply as 'Cassino' in the case of these two regiments only.

CASA SINAGOGGA

16th May, 1944

This was an important area in the German defences. It was captured after hard fighting in this subsidiary Engagement.

The Honour has been awarded to the:-

London Irish Rifles

LIRI VALLEY

189th to 30th May, 1944

In this Battle, XIII Corps and I Canadian Corps drove the enemy northwards from Cassino.

The Honour is borne on the Guidons of the:-

16th/5th Lancers	Royal Wiltshire Yeomanry

and has also been awarded to the:-

Derbyshire Yeomanry	Royal West Kent Regiment
Lothians and Border Horse	Royal Irish Fusiliers
North Irish Horse	Argyll and Sutherland Highlanders
Welsh Guards	Rifle Brigade
Buffs	London Irish Rifles
Royal Inniskilling Fusiliers	Tower Hamlets Rifles
Black Watch	Kensington Regiment

HITLER LINE

18th to 24th May, 1944

Primarily a Canadian operation, supported by 25th Tank Brigade, the troops in this subsidiary action included elements of the 4th, 78th and 6th Armoured Divisions. The attack broke the Hitler Line.

The Honour is borne on the Guidon of the:-

North Irish Horse

AQUINO

18th to 24th May, 1944

In this subsidiary action, there was an initial and unsuccessful attempt to advance in the Aquino area by XIII Corps. Thereafter, the corps maintained its positions, while the main attack was made by the Canadians.

The Honour has been awarded to the:-

Derbyshire Yeomanry	Argyll and Sutherland Highlanders
Buffs	

MELFA CROSSING

24th to 25th May, 1944

The River Melfa was the last German main line of defence in the Battle of the Liri Valley. In this subsidiary action, the main fighting was done by the Canadians.

The Honour has been awarded to the:-

    Rifle Brigade   Tower Hamlets Rifles

MONTE PICCOLO

26th to 28th May, 1944

1st Guards, and 26th Armoured Brigades, were involved in this subsidiary action in which this dominating position was captured and held.

The Honour is borne on the Colours of the:-

    Welsh Guards

and has also been awarded to the:-

    Coldstream Guards   17th/21st Lancers
    16th/5th Lancers   Lothians and Border Horse

ROME

22nd May to 4th June, 1944

The main attack direct towards Rome was made by the Fifth U.S. Army, with the French and British formations operating on the right and left flanks respectively. Thus it is that the only British troops to participate in this Battle were those of 1st and 5th Divisions breaking out of the Anzio beach-head.

The Honour was emblazoned by the:-

    Yorkshire Dragoons   Wiltshire Regiment
    Cheshire Regiment   North Staffordshire Regiment

and was also awarded to the:-

    Buffs   Duke of Wellington's Regiment
    Royal Inniskilling Fusiliers   Loyal Regiment
                                              Gordon Highlanders

ADVANCE TO TIBER

22nd May to 4th June, 1944

In this subsidiary action, 1st and 5th Divisions were involved in sharp fighting at Pantoni, Aprilia, the Moletta River, and Andrea.

The Honour is borne on the Guidon of the:-

    Royal Wiltshire Yeomanry

and has also been awarded to the:-

    Royal Scots Fusiliers   Wiltshire Regiment
    Cameronians   North Staffordshire Regiment
    Royal Inniskilling Fusiliers   York and Lancaster Regiment
    Sherwood Foresters

MONTE ROTONDO

6th to 7th June, 1944

6th Armoured Division fought this Engagement, during the pursuit after the fall of Rome. The strong points of Fonte di Papa and Monte Rotondo were taken in face of strong opposition.

The Honour has been awarded to the:-

    Lothians and Border Horse   Rifle Brigade

FICULLE

15th June, 1944

In this Engagement, the Warwickshire Yeomanry attacked and destroyed a determined rearguard of German parachute troops, losing 5 tanks.

The Honour is borne on the Guidon of the:-

    Warwickshire Yeomanry

MONTE GABBIONE

16th to 17th June, 1944

5/Northamptons captured this village, with tank and artillery support, after fierce house to house fighting.

The Honour has been awarded to the:-

    Northamptonshire Regiment

CITTA DELLA PIEVE

16th to 19th June, 1944

This Action, fought by 78th Division with 9th Armoured Brigade, resulted in the capture of an outpost position protecting the Trasimene Line.

The Honour is borne on the Guidons of the:-

    3rd Hussars   Royal Wiltshire Yeomanry

CAPTURE OF PERUGIA

18th to 29th June, 1944

1st Guards, 26th Armoured, and 61st Brigades were involved in this Action, under 6th Armoured Division. It resulted in the capture of an area which was a serious threat to the Trasimene Line.

The Honour is borne on the Guidon and Appointments of the:-

    17th/21st Lancers   Tower Hamlets Rifles
    Rifle Brigade

and has also been awarded to the:-

    King's Dragoons Guards   Coldstream Guards
    16th/5th Lancers   Welsh Guards
    Lothians and Border Horse

RIPA RIDGE

18th to 19th June, 1944

In this Engagement, 17th Indian Brigade attacked the ridge which extended for five miles between the Tiber and Chiascio rivers, and on which the villages of Ripa and Civitella d'Arno stood. It was captured after hard fighting.

The Honour has been awarded to the:-
> Royal Fusiliers

MONTE MALBE

19th to 20th June, 1944

7/R.B., supported by a squadron of 17/21 Lancers, were involved in fierce fighting during enemy counter-attacks after the position had been seized after a night advance of more than five miles. The enemy was completely defeated with the support of armour and artillery.

The Honour is borne on the Appointments of the:-
> London Rifle Brigade

and was also awarded to the:-
> Rifle Brigade

TRASIMENE LINE

20th to 30th June, 1944

This Battle involved the destruction of a strong German line which protected the Gothic Line. The battle was hard fought, and involved much close quarter fighting by the troops of XIII Corps (6th South African Armoured Division, with 24th Guards Brigade under command, 4th Division, with 10th, 12th, 28th, and 1st Canadian Armoured Brigades under command, and 78th Division, with 11th, 36th, 38th Infantry and 9th Armoured Brigades).

The Honour was emblazoned by the:-

Royal Wiltshire Yeomanry	Bedfordshire and Hertfordshire Regiment
Warwickshire Yeomanry	Royal West Kent Regiment
King's Regiment	

and was also awarded to the:-

Scots Guards	Duke of Cornwall's Light Infantry
Buffs	Royal Hampshire Regiment
Somerset Light Infantry	Northamptonshire Regiment
Lancashire Fusiliers	Royal Irish Fusiliers
Royal Inniskilling Fusiliers	London Irish Rifles

SANFATUCCHIO

20th to 21st June, 1944

In this subsidiary Engagement, troops of 78th Division captured this important position after bitterly contested fighting.

The Honour is borne on the Guidon of the:-

    Warwickshire Yeomanry

and has also been awarded to the:-

    London Irish Rifles

GABBIANO

1st July, 1944

In this Engagement, 2/Royal Fusiliers advanced in face of heavy fire from enemy infantry, mortars and artillery, and captured this strong position.

The Honour has been awarded to the:-

    Royal Fusiliers

AREZZO

4th to 17th July, 1944

This Battle was fought by XIII Corps: 6th Armoured Division (26th Armoured, 1st Guards and 61st Brigades), 6th South African Armoured Division (with 24th Guards Brigade under command), 4th Division (10th, 12th, 28th Brigades), 2nd New Zealand Division, and 'Sackforce' (improvised force consisting of King's Dragoons Guards, 1/King's Royal Rifle Corps, and 1/Argyll and Sutherland Highlanders). The scene of the Battle was an important outpost of the Gothic Line, and its capture gave Eighth Army a firm base for further advances.

The Honour has been awarded to the:-

Life Guards	Welsh Guards
Royal Horse Guards	Somerset Light Infantry
King's Dragoons Guards	Royal West Kent Regiment
16th/5th Lancers	King's Royal Rifle Corps
Derbyshire Yeomanry	Rifle Brigade
Lothians and Border Horse	London Rifle Brigade
Coldstream Guards	Tower Hamlets Rifles

TUORI

5th July, 1944

2/King's, in 28th Brigade, supported by Canadian tanks, captured this position after sharp fighting in this subsidiary Engagement, and held it in face of repeated counter-attacks and shelling, thus enabling the advance to continue.

The Honour was emblazoned by the:-

    King's Regiment

ADVANCE TO FLORENCE

17th July to 10th August, 1944

In this Battle, XIII Corps had to fight continuously against strong rearguard positions in the valley of the Middle Arno, and in the Chianti Hills to the west of it. The successful conclusion of these operations placed the Allied forces in a position to attack the Gothic Line. 6th Armoured, 6th South African Armoured, 4th, 78th, 2nd New Zealand and 8th Indian Divisions, and 25th Tank and 1st Canadian Armoured Brigades took part.

The Honour is borne on the Guidons of the:-

  16th/5th Lancers   Warwickshire Yeomanry
  Royal Wiltshire Yeomanry   North Irish Horse

and has also been awarded to the:-

  Life Guards   Royal Fusiliers
  Royal Horse Guards   Somerset Light Infantry
  17/21 Lancers   Duke of Cornwall's Light Infantry
  Derbyshire Yeomanry   Royal Hampshire Regiment
  Royal Tank Regiment   Black Watch
  Lothians and Border Horse   Royal West Kent Regiment
  Coldstream Guards   Rifle Brigade
  Scots Guards   Tower Hamlets Rifles
  Welsh Guards

MONTE SAN MICHELE

18th to 20th July, 1944

In this subsidiary action, 6th South African Armoured Division captured the mountain position after sharp fighting.

The Honour has been awarded to the:-

  Scots Guards

MONTE DOMINI

21st to 24th July, 1944

After attacks by 24th Guards Brigade, supported by South African tanks, for two days which only achieved partial success, the position was captured on the 23rd July in face of strong opposition in this subsidiary Engagement.

The Honour has been awarded to the:-

  Coldstream Guards

MONTE SCALARI

27th to 30th July, 1944

This was a key position in the German outpost line south of Florence. After hard fighting by 12th Brigade in this subsidiary engagement, with heavy casualties, the mountain was captured.

The Honour has been awarded to the:-

  Royal Fusiliers   Royal West Kent Regiment
  Black Watch

INCONTRO

5th to 8th August, 1944

In this final subsidiary action of the Battle for Florence, 4th Division, after severe fighting, captured Incontro, and thus caused the collapse of the enemy line.

The Honour was emblazoned by the:-

    Duke of Cornwall's Light Infantry

MONTONE

5th to 7th July, 1944

This Engagement was fought by 25th Indian Brigade. Montone was a strong position in the Tiber Valley. Its capture enabled 10th Indian Division to continue the advance northwards.

The Honour was emblazoned by the:-

    King's Own Royal Regiment

MONTE CEDRONE

13th to 18th July, 1944

In this Engagement, 10th Indian Brigade, with armoured support, seized this strong position which covered Citta di Castello.

The Honour is borne on the Guidon of the:-

    Royal Wiltshire Yeomanry

CITTA DI CASTELLO

16th to 22nd July, 1944

25th Indian Brigade fought this Engagement in which the attack was led by 1/King's Own and 3/18 Royal Garwhal Rifles. Later, the 3rd Hussars, after a sharp fight, captured the ridge immediately south of the town.

The Honour was emblazoned by the:-

    3rd Hussars   Royal Wiltshire Yeomanry

and has also been awarded to the:-

    King's Own Royal Regiment

PIAN DI MAGGIO

19th to 20th July, 1944

In this Engagement, the 1/2nd Gurkha Rifles made a night attack over difficult mountain country against strongly held positions. Sharp fighting led to the capture of the flanks of the objective; next morning, the whole position, with support of tanks, had been secured and repeated counter-attacks were defeated.

The Honour has been awarded to the:-

    2nd Gurkha Rifles

CAMPRIANO

20th to 28th July, 1944

11th Indian Brigade (2/7 Gurkha Rifles, 3/12 Frontier Force Regt.), captured this strong position, dominating a lateral road north of Arezzo, in this Engagement.

The Honour is borne on the Guidon of the:-

Warwickshire Yeomanry

and has also been awarded to the:-

7th Gurkha Rifles

CITERNA

25th to 26th July, 1944

In this Action, the attack by 10th Indian Division led to the capture of the area, and the withdrawal of the enemy on the whole of the X Corps front.

The Honour has been awarded to the:-

12th Lancers

POGGIO DEL GRILLO

4th to 8th August, 1944

This Engagement was the scene of heavy fighting by 11th Indian Brigade, supported by the Central India Horse. 2/Camerons captured Ferrato and Bibbiano, and one company captured Poggio del Grillo, but was heavily counter-attacked. The place was finally captured by 2/7 Gurkha Rifles.

The Honour is borne on the Appointments of the:-

7th Gurkha Rifles

and has also been awarded to the:-

Cameron Highlanders

FIESOLE

25th August, 1944

In this Engagement, 1/Loyals were involved in a fierce clash with the enemy on the high ground Ceceri-Fiesole beyond Florence.

The Honour is borne on the Colours of the:-

Loyal Regiment

MONTORSOLI

1st to 5th September, 1944

In this Engagement, 66th Brigade of 1st Division had some sharp fighting at Trespiano, Caldine, and Montorsoli while clearing the area north-east of Florence.

The Honour is borne on the Colours of the:-

Hertfordshire Regiment

ANCONA

2nd to 18th July, 1944

7th Hussars were serving at this time under command of II Polish Corps. In this Action, the Poles successfully fought their way forward to capture the town.

The Honour was emblazoned by the:-

    7th Hussars

GOTHIC LINE

25th August to 22nd September, 1944

In this Battle, the Gothic Line was pierced and broken except in the small coastal sector on the U.S. front. Heavy casualties, bad weather, and lack of reinforcements combined to prevent full exploitation after the line had been destroyed.

The following formations were involved in this Battle.

Under command of Eighth Army:

I Canadian Corps -	(1st Canadian Division, 5th Canadian Armoured Division, 21st Army Tank Brigade and Household Cavalry Regiment);
V Corps -	(46th Division, 4th Indian Division, 56th Division, 25th Tank Brigade and 6/R.T.R.);
X Corps -	(10th Indian Division and 9th Armoured Brigade);
II Polish Corps -	(with 7/Hussars under command).

Under command of Fifth U.S. Army

XIII Corps -	(6th Armoured Division, 1st Division, 8th Indian Division, and 1st Canadian Armoured Brigade);
6th South African Armoured Division	(under command of IV U.S. Corps).

The Honour was emblazoned by the:-

King's Dragoon Guards	Royal Hampshire Regiment
27th Lancers	Sherwood Foresters
North Irish Horse	Manchester Regiment
Grenadier Guards	Cameron Highlanders
Royal Scots	2nd Gurkha Rifles
Royal Fusiliers	London Scottish
Royal Lincolnshire Regiment	Hertfordshire Regiment
Royal Leicestershire Regiment	Cheshire Regiment

and was also awarded to the:-

Life Guards	King's Shropshire Light Infantry
Royal Horse Guards	Middlesex Regiment
12th Lancers	North Staffordshire Regiment
Royal Tank Regiment	York and Lancaster Regiment

Welsh Guards
Queen's Royal Regiment
Royal Sussex Regiment
Loyal Regiment
Durham Light Infantry
Rifle Brigade
London Rifle Brigade

MONTE GRIDOLFO

30th August to 2nd September, 1944

This was a strong mountain position in the Gothic Line. In this subsidiary action the enemy resisted fiercely the attacks made by 46th Division.

The Honour has been awarded to the:-

Royal Lincolnshire Regiment
Royal Leicestershire Regiment
Royal Hampshire Regiment
Manchester Regiment

TAVOLETO

1st to 4th September, 1944

In this subsidiary engagement, 5th Indian Brigade (1/9 Gurkha Rifles, and 4/11 Sikh Regt.) and 11th Indian Brigade (2/Camerons and 2/7 Gurkhas) were involved in heavy attacks and counter-attacks before Tavoleto was finally captured.

The Honour is borne on the Appointments of the:-

7th Gurkha Rifles

and has also been awarded to the:-

Cameron Highlanders

MONTEGAUDIO

28th August, 1944

In this subsidiary engagement, the Hampshires captured this strong outpost position after fierce opposition.

The Honour has been awarded to the:-

Royal Hampshire Regiment

CORIANO

3rd to 15th September, 1944

1st Armoured Division, 5th Canadian Armoured Division, 46th, 56th and 4th Indian Divisions were all involved in this Battle.

Initially unsuccessful, and costly in casualties, the attack finally succeeded after heavy fighting.

The Honour was emblazoned by the:-

Queen's Bays
4th Hussars
10th Hussars
Honourable Artillery Company
Royal Fusiliers
Sherwood Foresters
10th Gurkha Rifles
London Scottish

and was also awarded to the:-

- 9th Lancers
- Royal Tank Regiment
- Yorkshire Dragoons
- Buffs
- Cheshire Regiment
- Royal Hampshire Regiment
- Welch Regiment
- Oxfordshire and Buckinghamshire Light Infantry
- King's Royal Rifle Corps
- Manchester Regiment
- York and Lancaster Regiment
- Cameron Highlanders
- 2nd Gurkha Rifles
- 6th Gurkha Rifles
- London Irish Rifles

SAN CLEMENTE

3rd to 4th September, 1943

This subsidiary action, which was fought by 46th Division, included the high ground of Sant Andria, and by its capture secured the crossings over the River Conca.

The Honour has been awarded to the:-

- 4th Hussars
- Manchester Regiment
- York and Lancaster Regiment

POGGIO SAN GIOVANNI

3rd to 5th September, 1944

7th Indian Brigade (1/2 Gurkhas, 2/11 Sikhs) was involved in this subsidiary engagement, in which the way was cleared towards Pian di Castello.

The Honour has been awarded to the:-

- 2nd Gurkha Rifles

PIAN DI CASTELLO

5th to 8th September, 1944

This was an arduous subsidiary action in difficult hill country. 4th Indian Division, with 6/R.T.R. supporting, did the fighting.

The Honour has been awarded to the:-

- Royal Sussex Regiment
- Cameron Highlanders

CROCE

5th to 9th September, 1944

The fighting in this subsidiary action was exceedingly bitter, and Croce changed hands five times. After much confused fighting by 56th Division, with the support of 7th Armoured Brigade, the sector was held.

The Honour is borne on the Colours of the:-

- Welch Regiment

and has also been awarded to the:-

- Royal Fusiliers
- London Scottish
- London Irish Rifles

GEMMANO RIDGE

5th to 15th September, 1944

This was a subsidiary action of the Battle of Coriano. 169th Brigade of 56th Division, 138th and 139th Brigades of 46th Division, 2/Camerons of 11th Indian Brigade and 7/Oxf. Bucks. of 167th Brigade were involved. Opposition in all phases of the fighting was extremely fierce.

The Honour was emblazoned by the:-

    Queen's Royal Regiment   King's Own Yorkshire Light Infantry
    Oxfordshire and Buckinghamshire Light Infantry

and was also awarded to the:-

    Royal Lincolnshire Regiment   York and Lancaster Regiment
    Cheshire Regiment   Durham Light Infantry
    Manchester Regiment

MONTEBELLO-SCORTICATA RIDGE

22nd to 24th September, 1944

11th Indian Brigade (2/Camerons, 3/12 Frontier Force Regt. and 2/7 Gurkha Rifles) were involved in this Engagement, in which a strong mountain position overlooking the River Marecchia was captured after hard fighting.

The Honour has been awarded to the:-

    7th Gurkha Rifles

SANTARCANGELO

22nd to 24th September, 1944

In this Engagement, 43rd Gurkha Lorried Infantry Brigade (2/6, 2/8 and 2/10 Gurkhas with 10/Hussars) captured this strong position, and enabled the advance to continue.

The Honour is borne on the Guidon and Appointments of the:-

    10th Hussars   10th Gurkha Rifles

and has also been awarded to the:-

    6th Gurkha Rifles

MONTE REGGIANO

24th September to 1st October, 1944

In this Engagement 7th Indian Brigade captured Trebbio, Cornacchiara and Tribola. Finally, 2/11 Sikhs and 2/Camerons (from 11th Indian Brigade) captured Monte Reggiano. The fighting had been severe.

The Honour has been awarded to the:-

    Royal Sussex Regiment   2nd Gurkha Rifles
    Cameron Highlanders

SAVIGNANO

27th to 30th September, 1944

169th Brigade captured Savignano and Castelvecchio Ridge in this Engagement, overcoming strong opposition.

The Honour has been awarded to the:-

Cheshire Regiment

SAN MARTINO SOGLIANO

4th to 5th October, 1944.

In this Action, 10th Indian Division took all its objectives after fierce fighting and counter-attacks.

The Honour has been awarded to the:-

King's Own Royal Regiment

MONTE FARNETO

6th to 7th October, 1944

In this Engagement, 20th Indian Brigade supported by N.I.H. and 1/R.N.F. captured a strong position in difficult country, leading to the collapse of a sector held by two German divisions.

The Honour has been awarded to the:-

North Irish Horse

MONTILGALLO

7th to 8th October, 1944

128th Brigade attacked, in this Engagement, with tank support in face of particularly heavy opposition. Their success established 46th Division firmly across the River Fiumicino.

The Honour has been awarded to the:-

Royal Hampshire Regiment   Manchester Regiment

CARPINETA

12th to 15th October, 1944

138th Brigade captured this important communications centre south of Cesena after hard fighting, in this Engagement.

The Honour has been awarded to the:-

Queen's Bays   York and Lancaster Regiment
King's Own Yorkshire Light Infantry

MONTE CHICCO

13th to 14th October, 1944

In this Engagement , 43rd Gurkha Lorried Infantry Brigade captured and held the area including Monteguzzo. The bulk of the fighting was done by 2/6 Gurkha Rifles.

The Honour is borne on the Appointments of the:-

    6th Gurkha Rifles

MONTE CAVALLO
21st to 23rd October, 1944

This was a key position between the rivers Ronco and Savio. Its capture in this Action by 10th Indian Division, after hard fighting, led to a general enemy withdrawal in this area.

The Honour has been awarded to the:-

    North Irish Horse

CAPTURE OF FORLI
7th to 9th November, 1944

4th and 46th Divisions were involved in this hard fought Action, in which the enemy suffered severe losses.

The Honour was emblazoned by the:-

    King's Regiment

and was also awarded to the:-

9th Lancers	East Surrey Regiment
12th Lancers	Royal Hampshire Regiment
Somerset Light Infantry	Manchester Regiment

CASA FORTIS
9th to 11th November, 1944

This Engagement involved 12th Brigade in the house to house clearing of Forli after its capture.

The Honour is borne on the Guidon of the:-

    North Irish Horse

and has also been awarded to the:-

Royal Fusiliers	Royal West Kent Regiment
Black Watch	

COSINA CANAL CROSSING
20th to 23rd November, 1944

This Action was an operation carried out by 4th and 46th Divisions to established bridgeheads in face of strong opposition and counter-attacks. Its success caused the Germans to retire rapidly to the Lamone.

The Honour was emblazoned by the:-

    Somerset Light Infantry

and was also awarded to the:-

10th Hussars	Sherwood Foresters
Royal Hampshire Regiment	Durham Light Infantry

CASA BETTINI

24th November to 1st December, 1944

In this Action, 10th Indian Division carried out three attacks on this objective before they were finally successful. 10th and 20th Indian Brigades with 6/R.T.R., were involved.

The Honour has been awarded to the:-

North Irish Horse

LAMONE CROSSING

2nd to 13th December, 1944

The following troop were involved in this Battle. I Canadian Corps (5th Canadian Armoured Division, and 1st Canadian Division), 21st Tank Brigade (12/R.T.R., and 48/R.T.R.), 43rd Gurkha Lorried Infantry Brigade, V Corps (46th and 56th Divisions, 2nd New Zealand Division, 10th Indian Division, and 2nd Armoured Brigade), and II Polish Corps.

V Corps began the attack, and the crossing was quickly made under heavy fire, firm bridgeheads were established, and held against armoured counter-attacks. Despite strong opposition, the bridgehead was firm by the 13th December.

The Honour was emblazoned by the:-

Queen's Bays

and was also awarded to the:-

9th Lancers	Manchester Regiment
North Irish Horse	York and Lancaster Regiment
Royal Tank Regiment	6th Gurkha Rifles
Royal Lincolnshire Regiment	King's Royal Rifle Corps
Royal Hampshire Regiment	

PIDEURA

4th to 7th December, 1944

Fierce fighting in difficult country signalised this subsidiary engagement. This dominating area was captured and held, against four counter-attacks, by 128th Brigade.

The Honour has been awarded to the:-

9th Lancers	Royal Hampshire Regiment

DEFENCE OF LAMONE BRIDGEHEAD

9th December, 1944

46th Division, with 169th and 25th Indian Brigades under command, and armoured support, fought this severe Action, in which an intense artillery bombardment was followed by an attack supported by tanks, with the intention of destroying the bridgehead. The fighting continued all day until nightfall, and was a heavy defeat for the enemy.

The Honour was emblazoned by the:-

9th Lancers	King's Own Royal Regiment

and was also awarded to the:-

    Queen's Bays   Manchester Regiment
    King's Own Yorkshire Light Infantry   York and Lancaster Regiment

PERGOLA RIDGE

14th to 16th December, 1944

In this Action, 10th Indian, and 25th Indian Brigades, were concerned in the capture of this ridge of great tactical importance.

The Honour was awarded to the:-

    Durham Light Infantry

SENIO POCKET

4th to 5th January, 1945

This was a strongly held area east of the River Senio, and north of Faenza. It was necessary to capture it preparatory to attacking the Senio Line. The operation was successfully carried out by 167th Brigade and 7th Armoured Brigade in this Action.

The Honour was emblazoned by the:-

    4th Hussars

and was also awarded to the:-

    10th Hussars   London Scottish
    Queen's Royal Regiment

SENIO FLOODBANK

23rd February to 3rd March, 1945

This Action was an attack by 56th Division, with 43rd Gurkha Lorried Infantry Brigade under command, to secure the Senio floodbank in the Cotignola sector. The greater part of the floodbank was finally taken after very hard fighting.

The Honour was awarded to the:-

    Queen's Royal Regiment   6th Gurkha Rifles
    Cheshire Regiment   10th Gurkha Rifles
    London Irish Rifles

RIMINI LINE

14th to 21st September, 1944

In this Battle, the following troops were involved. I Canadian Corps (1st Canadian Division, 5th Canadian Armoured Division), and the following British formations: 1st Armoured Division, 4th, 46th and 56th Divisions, 4th Indian Division, 21st Tank Brigade (12/R.T.R., 48/R.T.R., 145/R.A.C.) 25th Tank Brigade (N.I.H., 51/R.T.R., 142/R.A.C.), and 3rd Greek Mountain Brigade.

Advancing over the River Conca, these formations successfully drove the enemy from three well-prepared positions on commanding ground, forcing him to retire across the Marecchia River.

The Honour was emblazoned by the:-

Queen's Bays	King's Regiment
4th Hussars	London Scottish
7th Hussars	London Irish Rifles
Yorkshire Dragoons	

and was also awarded to the:-

Royal Tank Regiment	Royal West Kent Regiment
Cheshire Regiment	Manchester Regiment
Duke of Cornwall's Light Infantry	York and Lancaster Regiment
Royal Hampshire Regiment	Cameron Highlanders
Welch Regiment	
Black Watch	

MONTE COLOMBO

14th September, 1944

In this subsidiary engagement, 2/5 Leicesters, with 'A' Squadron 142/R.A.C., attacked against strong opposition, finally securing their objective with 150 prisoners, two Panther tanks, and one self-propelled gun.

The Honour was awarded to the:-

Royal Leicestershire Regiment

CASA FABBRI RIDGE

14th September, 1944

In this subsidiary engagement, 12th Brigade (4th Division) took their objectives after stiff resistance from enemy infantry, tanks, and supporting arms, and repelled strong counter-attacks, thereby enabling the division to advance across the River Marano.

The Honour was awarded to the:-

Queen's Royal Regiment	Black Watch

MONTESCUDO

14th to 17th September, 1944

128th Brigade in 46th Division, captured this position, strongly held by the enemy, after four days' heavy fighting. Over 260 casualties were suffered by the three Hampshire battalions in this subsidiary engagement.

The Honour has been awarded to the:-

Royal Hampshire Regiment	Manchester Regiment

FRISONI

16th to 18th September, 1944

In this subsidiary engagement, 28th Brigade (4th Division) finally captured the area, which included a dominating ridge, after initial heavy counter-attacks had driven them back.

The Honour has been awarded to the:-

    Royal Hampshire Regiment

SAN MARINO

17th to 20th September, 1944

In this subsidiary action, 5th Indian Infantry Brigade, with 2/Camerons of 11th Indian Brigade, and 138th Brigade, fought a number of sharp engagements, and repulsed several German counter-attacks. The whole of the Republic had been captured by 20th September, thereby destroying the left flank of the Rimini Line position.

The Honour has been awarded to the:-

    Royal Lincolnshire Regiment   Cameron Highlanders
    York and Lancaster Regiment

CERIANO RIDGE

17th to 21st September, 1944

In this subsidiary action, V Corps employed 56th Division, with 7th Armoured Brigade and 1st Armoured Division. Fighting took place across country and across the River Ausa to capture the high ground of Ceriano Ridge. The advance was strongly contested by the enemy, and our infantry, and tank losses were very high.

The Honour is borne on the Guidon of the:-

    Yorkshire Dragoons

and has also been awarded to the:-

    Queen's Bays   London Scottish
    Cheshire Regiment   London Irish Rifles
    Welch Regiment

CESENA

15th to 20th October, 1944

1st Canadian Division, 139th Brigade (46th Division), and 25th Indian Brigade (10th Indian Division) were involved in this Action. Cesena was an important communications centre. It was captured after hard fighting, and the enemy was forced to retire behind the Savio.

The Honour has been awarded to the:-

    Queen's Bays   Manchester Regiment
    10th Hussars   Durham Light Infantry

SAVIO BRIDGEHEAD

20th to 23rd October, 1944

The main fighting in this Engagement was undertaken by 2nd Canadian Brigade, who established and consolidated the bridgehead after heavy fighting.

The Honour was emblazoned by the:-

    27th Lancers

and has also been awarded to the:-

    Royal Fusiliers   Black Watch
    Royal West Kent Regiment

CAPTURE OF RAVENNA

3rd to 4th December, 1944

In this Action, 5th Canadian Armoured Division and 'Porterforce' took part in some sharp fighting which forced the enemy to withdraw from Ravenna.

The Honour was emblazoned by the:-

    27th Lancers

CONVENTELLO-COMACCHIO

2nd to 6th January, 1945

This was a hard-fought Action in which 5th Canadian Armoured Division, 11th and 12th Canadian Brigades, with three British units attached, cleared the enemy between Valli di Comacchio and Conventello.

The Honour has been awarded to the:-

    4th Hussars   12th Lancers

MARRADI

21st to 24th September, 1944

This Action was fought by 1st Division. 2nd and 66th Brigades advanced through most difficult mountain terrain, and succeeded in destroying the position.

The Honour was emblazoned by the:-

    North Staffordshire Regiment

and was also awarded to the:-

    Royal Scots

MONTE GAMBERALDI

25th to 29th September, 1944

In this Action, 1st Division attacked this very strong position give times without success on the 25th and 26th September. It was finally captured on the 29th.

The Honour was emblazoned by the:-

    Hertfordshire Regiment

and was also awarded to the:-

    Royal Scots   Loyal Regiment

BATTAGLIA

2nd to 12th October, 1944

1st Guards Brigade, in this Engagement, held this mountain position against strong counter-attacks.

The Honour is borne on the Colours of the:-
Welsh Guards

and has also been awarded to the:-
Grenadier Guards

MONTE CASALINO

2nd to 23rd October, 1944

This was a strong enemy hill position which blocked the advance of 8th Indian Division. The Engagement comprised hard fighting until the position was finally captured by 1/5 R. Gurkha Rifles

The Honour has been awarded to the:-
Argyll and Sutherland Highlanders

MONTE CECO

3rd to 17th October, 1944

This Action, by 1st Division, involved the capture, and retention against heavy counter-attacks, of this strong position.

The Honour is borne on the Colours of the:-

Duke of Wellington's Regiment	Hertfordshire Regiment

and was also awarded to the:-

Lancashire Fusiliers	Loyal Regiment
Sherwood Foresters	King's Shropshire Light Infantry

MONTE LA PIEVE

13th to 19th October, 1944

78th Division made four attacks on this strongly held mountain feature before they were finally successful.

The Honour has been awarded to the:-
Northamptonshire Regiment

MONTE PIANOERENO

17th to 23rd October, 1944

This Action was one of the hardest fought by 8th Indian Division in Italy. Fighting took place in a strongly held mountain sector where the enemy resisted to the last man in some of his positions.

The Honour has been awarded to the:-
Royal West Kent Regiment

MONTE SPADURO

19th to 24th October, 1944

In this Action, 78th Division captured the position after hard fighting over difficult terrain, and held it against more than four counter-attacks.

The Honour has been awarded to the:-

Buffs	Argyll and Sutherland Highlanders
Lancashire Fusiliers	London Irish Rifles
Royal Inniskilling Fusiliers	Kensington Regiment
Royal Irish Fusiliers	

ORSARA

25th to 26th October, 1944

In this Engagement, 7/R.B. captured and held this position which protected the German position in the Santerno Valley area. A strong counter-attack was repulsed on the 26th October.

The Honour has been awarded to the:-

Rifle Brigade London Rifle Brigade

MONTE GRANDE

1st November to 12th December, 1944

This Action was fought by 1st Division, with 19th Indian Brigade, of 8th Indian Division. This was an important mountain position, captured by 88th U.S. Division in October, and held by 1st Division against repeated counter-attacks.

The Honour is borne on the Colours of the:-

Loyal Regiment Hertfordshire Regiment

and has also been awarded to the:-

King's Shropshire Light Infantry	Argyll and Sutherland Highlanders
Middlesex Regiment	London Irish Rifles
Royal Irish Fusiliers	

TOSSIGNANO

12th to 16th December, 1944

In this Engagement, 61st Brigade (6th Armoured Division), fought under great difficulties imposed by the terrain. 2/R.B. gained a footing in the village, suffering heavy casualties. They defeated five counter-attacks, but efforts to reinforce the battalion were unsuccessful, and it was overwhelmed. The Brigade suffered over 230 casualties.

The Honour has been awarded to the:-

Rifle Brigade Tower Hamlets Rifles

CATARELTO RIDGE

28th September to 3rd October, 1944

In this Engagement, 24th Guards Brigade (6th South African Armoured Division) captured the ridge after hard fighting at a cost of over 130 casualties. This enabled the Division to continue its operations towards Bologna.

The Honour has been awarded to the:-

    Coldstream Guards   Scots Guards

VALLI DI COMACCHIO

1st to 8th April, 1945

This Action was a successful preliminary operation preparatory to the crossing of the Senio. Carried out by 56th Division (167th Brigade, 24th Guards Brigade and 2nd Commando Brigade) round the Lake of Comacchio, it resulted in the capture of over 1,000 prisoners and 28 guns.

The Honour was emblazoned by the:-

    10th Hussars   London Scottish
    Special Air Service Regiment

and has also been awarded to the:-

    North Irish Horse   London Irish Rifles
    Royal Fusiliers   Commando Association
    Cheshire Regiment

SENIO

9th to 12th April, 1945

In this Battle, fought by Eighth Army, the following troops took part:-

    Under V Corps -   8th Indian Division, 78th Division and 2nd N.Z. Division;
    II Polish Corps -   two Divisions; Cremona Combat Group.
    Under X Corps -   Fruili Group (Italian); Jewish Brigade

The Senio was crossed after fierce and bitter fighting, particularly on the 8th Indian Division's sector. On the 11th and 12th April, the Santerno was crossed, and the strong German line was decisively broken. British casualties were heavy; over 2,250 German prisoners were taken.

The Honour was emblazoned by the:-

    North Irish Horse

and has also been awarded to the:-

    4th Hussars   Lancashire Fusiliers
    Honourable Artillery Company   Royal West Kent Regiment
    Buffs   Argyll and Sutherland Highlanders
    Royal Fusiliers

SANTERNO CROSSING

11th to 12th April, 1945

In this subsidiary action, the Santerno was crossed after hard fighting, and a bridgehead formed and held against strong counter-attacks. The crossing of this obstacle completed the destruction of the Senio position, and enabled Eighth Army to advance towards Argenta and the Bologna plain.

The Honour has been awarded to the:-

    4th Hussars   Argyll and Sutherland Highlanders

MENATE

10th to 11th April, 1945

This partly amphibious Engagement was carried out by 167th Brigade, with 40 (Royal Marine) Commando, against strong opposition from infantry, tanks and artillery. It was completely successful, and materially assisted the operations in the Argenta Gap.

The Honour was emblazoned by the:-

    27th Lancers

and was also awarded to the:-

    Queen's Royal Regiment

FILO

12th to 14th April, 1945

169th Brigade conducted this Engagement over very difficult ground against enemy opposition of all arms which strongly contested the advance. Filo, which was an important German rearguard position, was finally captured.

The Honour was emblazoned by the:-

    27th Lancers

and was also awarded to the:-

    Queen's Royal Regiment

ARGENTA GAP

13th to 21st April, 1945

This was a V Corps Battle. 6th Armoured Division, 56th and 78th Divisions, 2nd Commando Brigade, 21st Tank Brigade, 2nd Armoured Brigade, elements of 25th Armoured Brigade, and the Cremona Group, took part.

The sector, strongly held by the enemy, blocked the advance of Eighth Army to the valley of the Po. The position was destroyed after fierce fighting.

The Honour is borne on the Standard, Guidons, Colours and Appointments of the:-

Queen's Bays	Lothians and Border Horse
4th Hussars	Buffs
9th Lancers	Lancashire Fusiliers
10th Hussars	Royal West Kent Regiment

    16th/5th Lancers
    17th/21st Lancers
    27th Lancers
    Derbyshire Yeomanry
    London Scottish
    London Irish Rifles
    Royal Irish Fusiliers
    Kensington Regiment

and has also been awarded to the:-

    Royal Tank Regiment
    Coldstream Guards
    Scots Guards
    Queen's Royal Regiment
    Royal Fusiliers
    Royal Inniskilling Fusiliers
    Welch Regiment
    Northamptonshire Regiment
    King's Royal Rifle Corps
    Argyll and Sutherland Highlanders
    Rifle Brigade
    Commando Association
    East Surrey Regiment
    London Rifle Brigade

FOSSA CEMBALINA

20th to 21st April, 1945

This subsidiary engagement, fought by 6th Armoured Division, entailed hard fighting to establish bridgeheads in the face of strong opposition, counter attacks were partly successful but the British Tanks eventually broke through to cut off the last line of escape of two German divisions.

The Honour was emblazoned by the:-

    London Rifle Brigade

and has also been awarded to the:-

    17th/21st Lancers
    Derbyshire Yeomanry
    Rifle Brigade

SAN NICOLO CANAL

21st April, 1945

In this subsidiary engagement, the 38th (Irish) Brigade, with 9th Lancers, and 10th Hussars, established a bridgehead over the canal in darkness, and subsequently made a deep advance against strong opposition.

The Honour has been awarded to the:-

    Royal Irish Fusiliers

BOLOGNA

14th to 21st April, 1945

This Battle was mainly carried out by Fifth U.S. Army. 6th South African Armoured Division fought under command of II U.S. Corps. The operations on the right flank of X, XIII and II Polish Corps, under Eighth Army, were an important contribution to the success of the Battle, which took place in the hills south of Bologna.

The Honour was emblazoned by the:-

    12th Lancers
    14th/20th Hussars
    27th Lancers
    10th Gurkha Rifles

SILLARO CROSSING

14th to 16th April, 1945

This subsidiary action was mainly fought by 2nd N.Z. Division, which captured and held the bridgehead against heavy counter-attacks by infantry and armour.

The Honour has been awarded to the:-
- 12th Lancers
- 10th Gurkha Rifles
- Durham Light Infantry

MEDICINA

16th April, 1945

In this subsidiary engagement, 43rd Gurkha Lorried Infantry Brigade, (operating under 2nd Polish Corps), after establishing a bridgehead over the Sillaro, reached and captured the town of Medicina. Fierce close quarter fighting took place with German paratroops.

The Honour was emblazoned by the:-
- 14th/20th Hussars
- 6th Gurkha Rifles

GAIANA CROSSING

17th to 19th April, 1945

2nd N.Z. Division, and 43rd Gurkha Lorried Infantry Brigade, took part in this subsidiary action. A successful night attack was made, and a bridgehead established, in face of heavy opposition, but the advance was maintained.

The Honour has been awarded to the:-
- 6th Gurkha Rifles
- 10th Gurkha Rifles

and is emblazoned by the:-
- 27th Lancers

IDICE BRIDGEHEAD

20th to 21st April, 1945

In this subsidiary engagement, 20th Indian Brigade (10th Indian Division), by capturing this bridgehead, after severe fighting, completed the destruction of the German defences of Bologna on their eastern flank.

The Honour has been awarded to the:- 12th Lancers

TRAGHETTO

19th to 20th April, 1945

In this Engagement, a mixed body of troops from 6th Armoured Division, comprising 16th/5th Lancers, 1/K.R.R.C., 'A' Squadron, Derbyshire Yeomanry, and a troop of 104/R.H.A., attacked towards Traghetto in order to establish a bridgehead across the Po Morte di Primaro Canal. By 20th April, the attack had been successful, 300 prisoners being taken.

The Honour has been awarded to the:-
- 16th/5th Lancers

GREECE, 1941 and 1944-45

The Theatre Honour of 'Greece, 1941' covering the period from 10th to 29th April, commemorates the brief and unhappy campaign when British Commonwealth forces were hurriedly sent to that country in the endeavour to prevent a German occupation, and in the end were compelled to evacuate the country before all the intended forces had been landed. The British force included the 6th Australian Division, the New Zealand Division, and the 1st British Armoured Brigade Group.

More than three years later, British troops returned to Greece to prevent the fall of that country into Communist control, and to re-establish order. Some unpleasant fighting occurred, mainly in Athens. This period, from 16th September, 1944, to 15th January, 1945, is commemorated in the second Theatre Honour.

One regiment alone had the distinction of being represented in both periods, and the **Honour 'Greece, 1941, '44-45,'** is borne on the Appointments of the:-

> King's Royal Rifle Corps

The Honour 'Greece, 1941' is borne on the Guidon, Standards and Appointments of the:-

> 4th Hussars Rangers
> Royal Tank Regiment

The Honour 'Greece, 1944-45' is borne on the Colours and Appointments of the:-

> Highland Light Infantry Queen's Westminsters

and has also been awarded to the:-

> King's Dragoon Guards Essex Regiment
> Royal Fusiliers Royal West Kent Regiment
> King's (Liverpool) Regiment Durham Light Infantry
> Somerset Light Infantry 2nd Gurkha Rifles
> Royal Hampshire Regiment Special Air Service Regiment
> East Surrey Regiment Command Association
> Bedfordshire and Hertfordshire Regiment Parachute Regiment
> Black Watch

VEVE

10th to 12th April, 1941

This was the first Action of the campaign, in which the German thrust through the Monastir Gap was delayed. 19th Australian Infantry, 1st British Armoured Brigade, 27th New Zealand Machine-Gun Battalion and the 20th Greek Division, were involved.

The Honour is borne on the Appointments of the:-

> Rangers

whose 1st Battalion took part, and has also been awarded to the:-

> King's Royal Rifle Corps

PROASTEION
13th April, 1941

This was a delaying Engagement fought by the 1st British Armoured Brigade with New Zealand machine-gunners, during the withdrawal from Veve.

The Honour is borne on the Guidon and Appointments of the:-

    4th Hussars   Rangers

CORINTH CANAL
26th April, 1941

In this Engagement, air bombardment and German parachutists overwhelmed the British, Australian and New Zealand elements who were in the area.

The Honour is borne on the Guidon of the:-

    4th Hussars

ATHENS
2nd December, 1944 to 15th January, 1945

The name of this Action is borne on the Colours and Appointments of the:-

    King's (Liverpool Regiment   Queen's Westminsters
    Parachute Regiment

and has also been awarded to the:-

    King's Dragoon Guards   Black Watch
    Royal Fusiliers   Essex Regiment
    Somerset Light Infantry   Durham Light Infantry
    Royal Hampshire Regiment   Highland Light Infantry
    Bedfordshire and Hertfordshire Regiment

MIDDLE EAST, 1941-44

This Theatre covered operations not falling within the sphere of a land campaign in the area, which, operationally, included North Africa, Greece, Syria, Iraq, British Somaliland, and Abyssinia. The campaigns in these countries are however, separately dealt with as Theatres on their own.

'Middle East, 1941' is borne on the Appointments of the:-

    Rangers

and was also awarded to the:-

    Welch Regiment
    Black Watch
    King's Royal Rifle Corps
    York and Lancaster Regiment
    Argyll and Sutherland Highlanders

'Middle East, 1942' is borne on the Colours of the:-

    Northern Rhodesia Regiment

and was also awarded to the:-

    Royal Scots Fusiliers
    Royal Welch Fusiliers
    Royal Inniskilling Fusiliers
    South Lancashire Regiment
    Wiltshire Regiment
    Seaforth Highlanders
    King's African Rifles

'Middle East, 1943-44' has been emblazoned by the:-

    Special Air Service Regiment

'Middle East, 1943' was awarded to the:-

    Buffs
    Durham Light Infantry

'Middle East, 1944' was awarded to the:-

    Highland Light Infantry

CRETE

20th May to 1st June, 1941

This Battle was the gallant defence of the island in the first big airborne assault of the war.

The British Forces involved 2nd New Zealand Division, 14th British Brigade, 19th Australian Brigade, Mobile Naval Base Defence Organisation and Layforce (Commandos).

The Honour is borne on the Guidon and Colours of the:-

    3rd Hussars
    Royal Leicestershire Regiment
    Welch Regiment
    Black Watch
    York and Lancaster Regiment
    Argyll and Sutherland Highlanders
    Rangers

and was also awarded to the:-

    King's Royal Rifle Corps
    Commando Association

CANEA

20th to 27th May, 1941

In this subsidiary action, fierce fighting took place until the pressure from increasing landings of German forces compelled a withdrawal.

The Honour is borne on the Colours and Appointments of the:-
- Welch Regiment
- Rangers

HERAKLION

20th to 29th May, 1941

In this subsidiary action, 14th Brigade stubbornly defended the harbour until forced to withdraw.

The Honour was awarded to the:-
- Royal Leicestershire Regiment
- York and Lancaster Regiment
- Black Watch
- Argyll and Sutherland Highlanders

RETIMO

20th to 30th May, 1941

The main fighting in this Action was carried out by the 19th Australian Infantry Brigade in defence of Retimo Harbour. A gallant attempt was made by the Rangers to break through to the garrison, but it ended in failure.

The Honour was awarded to the:-
- Rangers

WITHDRAWAL to SPHAKIA

28th May to 1st June, 1941

In this subsidiary action, a hard withdrawal was followed by fighting and counter-attacks on the beach perimeter to cover the embarkation of the withdrawing troops.

The Honour has been awarded to the:-
- Welch Regiment

MADAGASCAR

5th May to 6th November, 1942

In this Action, Force 121 landed on the west coast in Courrier and Ambararata Bays, and attacked Diego Suarez overland. After severe fighting on the Bellevue-Caimans line, Diego Suarez capitulated on 8th May. Majunga was captured from the sea on 10th September. On 23rd September, the capital, Tananarive, was occupied.

The troops involved were 29th Independent Brigade, 13th and 17th Brigade (of 5th Division) and 5/Commando initially. 22nd East African Brigade came in later.

The Honour is borne on the Colours of the:-
- Royal Welch Fusiliers
- Seaforth Highlanders
- East Lancashire Regiment
- King's African Rifles
- South Lancashire Regiment

and was also awarded to the:-

    Royal Scots Fusiliers   Commando Association
    Northamptonshire Regiment

COS

3rd to 16th October, 1943

In this Engagement, 1/D.L.I. defended the island against German attack until the remnants of the battalion were evacuated.

The Honour was awarded to the:-
    Durham Light Infantry

LEROS

12th to 16th November, 1943

In this Engagement, the island was defended by 234th Brigade until the garrison was forced to surrender.

The Honour was emblazoned by the:-
    Buffs

and was also awarded to the:-
    Royal West Kent Regiment   Royal Irish Fusiliers

ADRIATIC

18th March to 21st November, 1944

This Action is made up of eight raids or attacks at Grohote, Hvar, Brac, Spilje, Sumartin, Solta, Sarande and Risan. All were undertaken in conjunction with the Jugo-Slav Partisans, in order to draw enemy forces to this flank. Some heavy fighting occurred, and considerable casualties were inflicted on the Germans.

The Honour was emblazoned by the:-
    Special Air Service Regiment

and was also awarded to the:-
    Highland Light Infantry   Commando Association

MALTA

11th June, 1940 to 20th November, 1942

Malta was never invaded, but the harbour was attacked by sea, and the whole island endured a very large number of bombing raids of varying intensity.

As a token of this successful defence, the island was awarded the George Cross.

As no ground operations took place during this period, the Theatre Honour only was awarded.

'Malta, 1940' was emblazoned by the:-

    Manchester Regiment   Royal Irish Fusiliers

'Malta, 1940-42' was emblazoned by the:-

    Devonshire Regiment   Royal West Kent Regiment
    Dorset Regiment   Malta Regiment

and was also awarded to the:-

    Buffs

'Malta, 1941-42' was emblazoned by the:-

    King's own Royal Regiment   Cheshire Regiment
    Lancashire Fusiliers   Royal Hampshire Regiment

'Malta, 1942' was awarded to the:-

    Durham Light Infantry

MALAYA, 1941-42

This comparatively short campaign, in which the Japanese (contrary to expectation) attacked overland and took Singapore Island in the rear, resulted in the rapid loss of Malaya.

'Malaya, 1941-42' was emblazoned by the:-

    Royal Leicestershire Regiment   Argyll and Sutherland Highlanders
    East Surrey Regiment   Malay Regiment

and was also awarded to the:-

    Loyal Regiment   2nd Gurkha Rifles
    Manchester Regiment

'Malaya, 1942' was emblazoned by the:-

    Cambridgeshire Regiment   Singapore Volunteer Corps

and was also awarded to the:-

    Royal Norfolk Regiment   Bedfordshire and Hertfordshire Regiment
    Suffolk Regiment   Sherwood Foresters

NORTH MALAYA

8th to 23rd December, 1941

This Battle, fought by III Indian Corps with 11th Indian Division and one brigade of 9th Indian Division, had for its immediate object the retention of control over the important airfields in North Malaya. III Indian Corps were defeated in the initial actions, and were afterwards forced back to Central Malaya by stages.

The Honour has been awarded to the:-

    Argyll and Sutherland Highlanders   2nd Gurkha Rifles

JITRA

10th to 13th December, 1941

This subsidiary action was fought on a semi-prepared position after the outpost troops had been almost entirely annihilated. The enemy penetrated into the position, and threatened the line of communication. The action developed into a running fight as far as Alor Star.

The Honour is borne on the Appointments of the:-

    2nd Gurkha Rifles

GRIK ROAD

17th to 23rd December, 1941

This subsidiary engagement involved a series of delaying engagements in protection of the line of communication bottle-neck at Kuala Kangsar, whilst the bulk of 11th Division withdrew across the River Perak. 2/A. & S.H. fought skilfully in these operations.

The Honour is borne on the Colours of the:-

    Argyll and Sutherland Highlanders

CENTRAL MALAYA

26th December, 1941 to 10th January, 1942

In this Battle, III Indian Corps (9th and 11th Indian Divisions) attempted to keep control of lateral communications between Kuantan, Kuala Lumpur and Port Swettenham. Their defeat at Slim River compelled withdrawal.

The Honour has been awarded to the:-

    Argyll and Sutherland Highlanders   2nd Gurkha Rifles

IPOH

26th to 29th December, 1941

Successful delaying operations took place in this subsidiary engagements.

The Honour has been awarded to the:-

    Argyll and Sutherland Highlanders

KAMPAR

30th December, 1941 to 3rd January, 1942

This subsidiary action provided the first opportunity since Jitra to fight in selected positions, considerably prepared. A practically unbroken front was maintained against Japanese attacks, but the arrival of another Japanese force to threaten the line of communication led to the withdrawal from Kampar of the 11th Indian Division.

The Honour was awarded to the:-

    Royal Leicestershire Regiment   2nd Gurkha Rifles
    East Surrey Regiment

SLIM RIVER

7th January, 1942

This disastrous subsidiary action finished 11th Indian Division as an effective formation, and spelt the loss of Kuala Lumpur. Japanese tanks broke through the battle-weary troops, and heavy losses occurred.

The Honour is borne on the Appointments of the:-

    2nd Gurkha Rifles

and was also awarded to the:-

    Argyll and Sutherland Highlanders

JOHORE

14th to 31st January, 1942

This Battle was fought by III Indian Corps (11th Indian Division, 9th Indian Division and 8th Australian Division) with the immediate object of retaining sufficient room on the mainland to deploy reinforcements when they arrived. Reverses at Muar, and at Batu Pahat, converted it into a hurried withdrawal across the causeway to Singapore Island.

The Honour is borne on the Colours of the:-

    Cambridgeshire Regiment   Loyal Regiment

and was also awarded to the:-

    Royal Norfolk Regiment   2nd Gurkha Rifles

MUAR

16th to 23rd January, 1942

9th Indian Division, 8th Australian Division (less one brigade), 45th Indian Brigade and 53rd Brigade took part in this subsidiary action. The extermination of 45th Indian Brigade and two reinforcing Australian battalions led to a withdrawal to Batu Pahat.

The Honour has been awarded to the:-

    Royal Norfolk Regiment

BATU PAHAT

21st to 26th January, 1942

This was an important, if isolated, bastion of the line of communications on the mainland. In this subsidiary action, endeavours to retain it resulted, after severe fighting, in the town being nearly surrounded, and the coastal road in rear being cut. A relieving force was itself surrounded, and the British forces were dispersed.

The Honour is borne on the Colours of the:-

    Cambridgeshire Regiment

and was also awarded to the:-

    Royal Norfolk Regiment   Loyal Regiment

SINGAPORE ISLAND

8th to 15th February, 1942

In this unhappy Battle, fought by Malaya Command (18th Division, 8th Australian Division, 11th Indian Division and Fortress Troops), confused fighting took place to retain possession of the island until its surrender.

The Honour was emblazoned by the:-

    Royal Norfolk Regiment   Cambridgeshire Regiment
    Suffolk Regiment   Malay Regiment
    Sherwood Foresters   Singapore Volunteer Corps
    Loyal Regiment

and was also awarded to the:-

    Royal Northumberland Fusiliers   Manchester Regiment
    Bedfordshire and Hertfordshire   Argyll and Sutherland Highlanders
        Regiment   2nd Gurkha Rifles

SOUTH-EAST ASIA, 1941

The fighting in this Theatre covered the loss of Hong Kong and British North Borneo.

'SOUTH-EAST ASIA, 1941' has been awarded to the:-

    Royal Scots
    Middlesex Regiment

HONG KONG
8th to 25th December, 1941

The fighting in this Action covered the defence of the Kowloon Peninsula, and the island of Hong Kong, until its surrender.

The Honour was emblazoned by the:-

    Middlesex Regiment

and was also awarded to the:-

    Hong Kong Volunteer Defence Corps

BURMA, 1942-45

The campaigns in Burma covered the period of the Japanese invasion, and consequent retreat across the Chindwin, of the Anglo-Indian forces, a year of minor operations on the Indo-Burmese border, and finally the reconquest of Burma with the overwhelming defeat of the enemy.

The Honour 'Burma, 1942-45' was emblazoned by the:-
    Royal Berkshire Regiment

and was also awarded to the:-
    West Yorkshire Regiment   10th Gurkha Rifles
    7th Gurkha Rifles

'Burma, 1942, '44-45,' is borne on the Colours of the:-
    Gloucestershire Regiment

'Burma, 1942,' was emblazoned by the:-
    7th Hussars   King's Own Yorkshire Light Infantry
    Royal Tank Regiment

'Burma, 1942-43,' is borne on the Colours of the:-
    Royal Inniskilling Fusiliers

'Burma, 1942-44,' was emblazoned by the:-
    Duke of Wellington's Regiment   Seaforth Highlanders

'Burma, 1942, 44,' is borne on the Appointments of the:-
    Cameronians

'Burma, 1943-45,' was emblazoned by the:-
    Royal Scots   Nigeria Regiment
    Royal Lincolnshire Regiment   Gold Coast Regiment
    Devonshire Regiment   Sierra Leone Regiment
    Suffolk Regiment   Gambia Regiment
    Lancashire Fusiliers
    Border Regiment
    Royal Sussex Regiment
    Northamptonshire Regiment

and was also awarded to the:-
    Queen's Royal Regiment   Royal West Kent Regiment
    Royal Welch Fusiliers   York and Lancaster Regiment
    South Lancashire Regiment   Durham Light Infantry
    Oxfordshire and Buckinghamshire Light Infantry   2nd Gurkha Rifles
    Essex Regiment   Commando Association

'Burma, 1943,' was emblazoned by the:-
    North Staffordshire Regiment

'Burma, 1943-44,' was awarded to the:-
    King's Regiment   Wiltshire Regiment
    Somerset Light Infantry

'**Burma, 1943, '45,**' was awarded to the:-
    King's Own Scottish Borderers.

'**Burma, 1944-45,**' was emblazoned by the:-

    25th Dragoons   6th Gurkha Rifles
    Royal Norfolk Regiment   King's African Rifles
    South Wales Borderers   Rhodesian African Rifles
    Worcestershire Regiment   North Rhodesia Regiment
    East Lancashire Regiment
    Welch Regiment

and was also awarded to the:-

    3rd Dragoon Guards   Cameron Highlanders
    Royal Scots Fusiliers
    Dorset Regiment
    Manchester Regiment

'**Burma, 1944,**' is borne on the Colours of the:-

    South Staffordshire Regiment   Black Watch

and was also awarded to the:-

    King's Own Royal Regiment   Bedfordshire and Hertfordshire Regiment

'**Burma, 1945,**' is borne on the Colours of the:-

    Royal Warwickshire Regiment   East Yorkshire Regiment

and was also awarded to the:-

    Buffs   Green Howards

SITTANG, 1942

16th to 23rd February

This Action was fought by 17th Indian Division, in order to hold the Japanese east of Rangoon, until reinforcements arrived. 16th Brigade held the Bilin River line, and with the aid of a battalion from 48th Brigade, resisted superior enemy forces on a front of 15 miles from the mouth of the river to Yunon. The withdrawal of the Division on 20th February, was closely followed up. The bridge over the Sittang was prematurely blown, and 16th and 46th Brigades were left, fighting desperately, on the wrong side.

The Honour is borne on the Colours and Appointments of the:-

    Duke of Wellington's Regiment   7th Gurkha Rifles (with 'Sittang, 1945')

and was also awarded to the:-

    King's Own Yorkshire Light Infantry

PEGU, 1942

6th to 7th March

This Action was fought by 48th Indian Brigade Group, during the withdrawal from Rangoon. Fierce hand-to-hand fighting took place at road blocks.

The Honour was emblazoned by the:-

    7th Hussars   West Yorkshire Regiment

and was also awarded to the:-

    Cameronians   7th Gurkha Rifles

TAUKYAN

7th to 8th March, 1942

In this Engagement, the enemy having blocked the road to Prome, attacks were made by 63rd Indian Brigade. The enemy withdrew, and the force continued withdrawing northwards.

The Honour is borne on the Colours of the:-

    Gloucestershire Regiment

PAUNGDE

28th to 30th March, 1942

In this offensive Action, undertaken to help relieve pressure on the Chinese 5th Army, 'Anstice Column' (equivalent of a brigade group) occupied Padigaon and Wetpok, but failed to capture Paungde, though inflicting considerable losses on the enemy.

The Honour was emblazoned by the:-

    7th Hussars   Gloucestershire Regiment

and was also awarded to the:-

    Cameronians   Duke of Wellington's Regiment

YENANGYAUNG, 1942

11th to 19th April

This Action was fought by Burma Corps (17th Indian Division, 1st Burma Division), to cover the destruction of the oilfields. While 17th Indian Division was strongly resisting enemy attacks in the area Thadodan-Kakkogwa, the Japanese, by seizing Migyaungye, exposed the right flank of 1st Burma Division, and withdrawal became inevitable. In the subsequent fighting, 1st Burma Division suffered heavy losses, and was greatly reduced in fighting value.

The Honour was emblazoned by the:-

    West Yorkshire Regiment   Royal Inniskilling Fusiliers

and was also awarded to the:-

    Cameronians

KYAUKSE, 1942

28th to 29th April.

48th Indian Brigade Group fought this Action with success to protect the crossing of the Irrawaddy by the British forces, and to allow time for two Chinese brigades to concentrate in the Mandalay area.

The Honour is borne on the Appointments of the:-

    7th Gurkha Rifles

MONYWA, 1942

30th April to 2nd May

In this Action, involving 1st Burma Division and 48th Indian Brigade, the Japanese placed a road block at Monywa in rear of 1st Burma Division. The block was eventually broken, and the withdrawal continued.

The Honour has been awarded to the:-

Gloucestershire Regiment   10th Gurkha Rifles

SHWEGYIN

9th to 11th May, 1942

In this Action, the Japanese caught up with the retreating 17th Indian Division at Shwegyin ferry, and fought hard to prevent embarkation. There were heavy losses on both sides.

The Honour has been awarded to the:-

7th Gurkha Rifles

RATHEDAUNG

29th December, 1942 to 3rd February, 1943

Throughout the period of this Action, 123rd Indian Brigade Group attacked unsuccessfully from Buthidaung in the attempt to capture Rathedaung. 10/L.F. were concerned in two of these attempts, in which hard fighting took place.

The Honour has been awarded to the:-

Lancashire Fusiliers

DONBAIK

8th January to 18th March, 1943

47th In, 55th Indian, 71st Indian and 6th Brigades, were all concerned at different times in this Action, in which some fierce and gallant attacks were made.

The Honour is borne on the Colours of the:-

Royal Welch Fusiliers

and was also awarded to the:-

Royal Scots   Royal Berkshire Regiment
Royal Lincolnshire Regiment   Durham Light Infantry
Royal Inniskilling Fusiliers

HTIZWE

6th to 16th March, 1943

In this Action, 123rd and 55th In Brigade Groups were subjected to ten days of close and wearing pressure, resulting in their withdrawal.

The Honour has been awarded to the:-

Lancashire Fusiliers

POINT 201 (ARAKAN)
28th to 29th March, 1943

This Engagement was a carefully planned raid by 71st Indian Brigade Group on a tactical feature occupied by the enemy. It was captured and held by 1/Lincolns.

The Honour has been awarded to the:-
    Royal Lincolnshire Regiment

YU
18th to 20th January, 1944

In this Engagement, 32nd Indian Brigade (1/Northants, 4/10 G.R., 3/8 G.R) attacked a Japanese stronghold near Kyaukchaw on the Yu river.

The Honour was emblazoned by the:-
    Northamptonshire Regiment

NORTH ARAKAN
1st January to 12th June, 1944

In this Battle, XV Corps (5th Indian, 7th Indian, 25th Indian, 26th Indian, 36th Indian and 81st West African Divisions and 3rd Special Service Brigade) was involved. In January, XV Corps advanced to capture the Maungdaw-Buthidaung road as a first step to the capture of Akyab. The Japanese launched a counter-offensive on 4th February, which was finally broken by 28th, but with the capture of the Tunnels fortress by the end of April, the Battle had to be concluded, although the Japanese continued the fighting for a further period.

The Honour was emblazoned by the:-

- 25th Dragoons
- Queen's Royal Regiment
- Suffolk Regiment
- Somerset Light Infantry
- Royal Scots Fusiliers
- Royal Welch Fusiliers
- South Lancashire Regiment
- Wiltshire Regiment
- York and Lancaster Regiment
- 2nd Gurkha Rifles
- Gold Coast Regiment
- Sierra Leone Regiment
- Gambia Regiment

and was also awarded to the:-

- Royal Lincolnshire Regiment
- West Yorkshire Regiment
- South Wales Borderers
- King's Own Scottish Borderers
- Gloucestershire Regiment
- East Lancashire Regiment
- Royal Sussex Regiment
- Royal West Kent Regiment
- Manchester Regiment
- Nigeria Regiment

BUTHIDAUNG

16th January to 3rd February and
5th March to 8th April, 1944

This subsidiary action, involving 7th Indian Division (33rd Indian, 89th Indian and 114th Indian Brigades), covered the first stages of the advance on the Buthidaung road. After a pause, due to the enemy's counter-offensive, the attack was resumed and objective captured.

The Honour was emblazoned by the:-

    25th Dragoons

and has been awarded to the:-

    Royal Lincolnshire Regiment   King's Own Scottish Borderers
    Somerset Light Infantry

RAZABIL

19th to 30th January, and
10th to 17th March, 1944

This subsidiary action involved 5th Indian Division (161st Indian, 123rd Indian and 9th Indian Brigades) and 29th Indian Brigade (36th Indian Division). Razabil was the very strong western bastion of the Mayu position. The first assault achieved only very limited success. In the second assault, the Japanese were driven out.

The Honour was emblazoned by the:-

    25th Dragoons

and has been awarded to the:-

    Royal Scots Fusiliers
    Royal West Kent Regiment

KALADAN

4th February to 31st March, 1944

81st West African Division (less 3rd W.A. Brigade) fought this subsidiary engagement, in which they advanced down the Kaladan valley and secured the Kyauktaw plan as far south as Apaukwa, covering the left flank of XV Corps' advance down the Majy Peninsula. In early March, a Japanese counter-offensive forced their withdrawal.

The Honour is borne on the Colours of the:-

    Nigeria Regiment   Sierra Leone Regiment
    Gold Coast Regiment   Gambia Regiment

POINT 551

3rd April to 22nd May, 1944

In this subsidiary action, 26th Indian Division, and 53rd Indian Brigade (9/Y. & L., 4/18 Garhwal Rif., 2/2 Punjab) 25th Indian Division were involved. Point 551 overlooked the eastern half of the Maungdaw-Buthidaung road. It was a vital defence locality, stubbornly clung to by the Japanese after they had lost the

Tunnels. It took a month to drive them off. This action includes the enemy counter-attack on Buthidaung in early May.

The Honour has been awarded to the:-

Wiltshire Regiment

ALETHANGYAW

8th March to 15th April, 1944

This subsidiary engagement was a Commando raid on the Arakan coast, undertaken to pin Japanese forces to coast defence, while XV Corps captured the Mayu fortress. 3rd Special Service Brigade (5 and 44(R.M) Commandos), carried out the raids from a base established by 81st (W.A) Reconnaissance Regiment.

The Honour has been awarded to the:-

Commando Association

MAYU TUNNELS

15th March to 20th April, 1944

25th Indian Division and 36th Indian Divisions achieved the capture of the Tunnels, and the peaks of the main Mayu range to north and south of the Maungdaw-Buthidaung road, in this subsidiary action.

The Honour was emblazoned by the:-

South Wales Borderers

and has also been awarded to the:-

Gloucestershire Regiment   Royal West Kent Regiment
South Lancashire Regiment   Wiltshire Regiment

MAUNGDAW

1st January to 31st May, 1944

This subsidiary engagement, involving 5th Indian and 25th Indian Divisions, and 3rd Special Service Brigade, records the long series of fights which included the capture, consolidation and defence of Maungdaw.

The Honour was emblazoned by the:-

West Yorkshire Regiment

and was also awarded to the:-

York and Lancaster Regiment

MOWDOK

3rd May to 12th June, 1944

6th (W.A) Brigade (4/Nigeria, 1/Gambia, 1/S.Leone) was heavily attacked, in this subsidiary engagement, in positions covering Mowdok.

The Honour is borne on the Colours of the:-

Gambia Regiment

NGAKYEDAUK PASS

4th February to 4th March, 1944

In this Battle, the Japanese attacked towards Chittagong, while their Fifteenth Army carried out its Imphal offensive. The enemy failed in their attempt to destroy 7th Indian Division after a month's fierce fighting. In addition to 7th Indian Division, elements of 5th and 26th Indian Divisions were involved.

The Honour was emblazoned by the:-

    25th Dragoons   King's Own Scottish Borderers
    Royal Lincolnshire Regiment
    Somerset Light Infantry

and was also awarded to the:-

    Wiltshire Regiment

DEFENCE OF SINZWEYA

5th to 29th February, 1944

In this subsidiary action, known at the time as the 'Battle of the Boxes,' 7th Indian Division, 9th Indian and 89th Indian Brigades, defended the Corps Maintenance Centre against continuous, heavy enemy attacks.

The Honour was emblazoned by the:-

    West Yorkshire Regiment

IMPHAL

12th March to 22nd June, 1944

This Battle, fought by IV Corps, took place when a major Japanese offensive was launched by their Fifteenth Army in the Chin Hills, up the Kabaw Valley, and across the Chindwin. Before this attack, IV Corps withdrew in accordance with previous plans, to the Imphal plain. There the Corps stood fighting until the remnants of Fifteenth Army withdrew.

The Honour is borne on the Colours and Appointments of the:-

3rd Dragoon Guards	Border Regiment
Devonshire Regiment	Northamptonshire Regiment
Suffolk Regiment	Seaforth Highlanders
West Yorkshire Regiment	7th Gurkha Rifles
King's Own Scottish Borderers	10th Gurkha Rifles

TUITUM

16th to 24th March, 1944

63rd Indian Brigade (1/3 G.R., 1/4 G.R., 1/10 G.R.) and 7/10 Baluch were involved in this subsidiary action: the attack, capture and subsequent defence of the Tuitum Ridge.

The Honour is borne on the Appointments of the:-

    10th Gurkha Rifles

SAKAWNG

18th to 25th March, 1944

This subsidiary action was the fight to clear the Mile 109 road block established by the Japanese behind 17th Indian Division. 48th Indian Brigade (9/Border, 2/5 R.G.R., 1/7 G.R.) with 1/W. Yorks and 4/12 F.F.Rrgt, and 37th Indian Brigade (3/3 G.R., 3/5 R.G.R., and 3/10 G.R.) with 9Jat, took part.

The Honour has been awarded to the:-

    Border Regiment

TAMU ROAD

12th March to 4th April, 1944

In this subsidiary action, rearguard actions were fought by 100th Indian Brigade (2/Border, 4/10 G.R.) and 3 D.G. near Witok, 32nd Indian Brigade around Moreh, and 80th Indian Brigade (1/Devon, 3/1 G.R., 9/12 F.F.Regt) towards Khongkang.

The Honour has been awarded to the:-

3rd Dragoon Guards	Northamptonshire Regiment
Devonshire Regiment	10th Gurkha Rifles
Border Regiment	

SHENAM PASS

1st April to 22nd June, 1944

In this subsidiary action, 20th Indian and 23rd Indian Divisions, were concerned with continuous and bitter fighting against the Japanese force trying to break into the Imphal plain along the Tamu-Palel road.

The Honour has been awarded to the:-

Devonshire Regiment	Seaforth Highlanders
Border Regiment	10th Gurkha Rifles

NUNSHIGUM

5th to 13th April, 1944

In this subsidiary action, the Japanese reached the nearest point to Imphal, and a fierce struggle for its possession ensued. The troops involved were 9th Indian Brigade, elements of 123rd Indian Brigade and 254th Indian Tank Brigade, 3/9 Jat, 1/17 Dogra, 2/W.Yorkshire, and 3 D.G.

The Honour is borne on the Standard of the:-

    3rd Dragoon Guards

LITAN

12th April to 15th May, 1944

This subsidiary action, fought by 23rd Indian Division, (1st Indian, 37th Indian, and 49th Indian Brigades), was an offensive to destroy H.Q., 15th Japanese Division, believed to be near Kasom.

The Honour was awarded to the:-

Seaforth Highlanders	10th Gurkha Rifles

BISHENPUR

14th April to 22nd June, 1944

In this subsidiary action, affecting 17th Indian Division and 32nd Indian Brigade (20th Indian Division), fighting raged round Bishenpur, 16 miles south-west of Imphal, on the Tiddim road. It included attacks and counter-attacks on Wireless Hill, Ningthoukong, Potsangbum and Bishenpur, which was important in lying at the junction of the Silchar track with the Tiddim road.

The Honour was emblazoned by the:-

    3rd Dragoon Guards   7th Gurkha Rifles
    West Yorkshire Regiment

and was also awarded to the:-

    Northamptonshire Regiment   10th Gurkha Rifles

KANGLATONGBI

21st April to 22nd June, 1944

5th Indian Division (less 161st Indian Brigade) and 89th Indian Brigade (7th Indian Division), took part in this subsidiary action, which covers the fight to recapture Kanglatongbi, and all the operations up the Imphal-Kohima road, until contact was made with 2nd Division.

The Honour is borne on the Standard of the:-

    3rd Dragoon Guards

and was also awarded to the:-

    West Yorkshire Regiment   King's Own Scottish Borderers

KOHIMA

27th March to 22nd June, 1944

In this Battle, fought by XXXIII Corps, the Japanese attacked the Kohima outposts at Jessami and Kharasom on the 29th March. Thereafter, the battle covered the Japanese attack on Kohima, and the counter-attack by XXXIII Corps, leading to the retreat of the enemy in disorder.

The Honour was emblazoned by the:-

    Royal Scots   Dorset Regiment
    Queen's Royal Regiment   South Lancashire Regiment
    Royal Norfolk Regiment   Royal Berkshire Regiment
    Lancashire Fusiliers   Manchester Regiment
    Royal Welch Fusiliers   Durham Light Infantry
    Worcestershire Regiment   Cameron Highlanders

and was also awarded to the:-

    Duke of Wellington's Regiment   Essex Regiment
    Border Regiment

DEFENCE OF KOHIMA

4th to 18th April, 1944

This small Kohima Garrison, which included 4/R.W.K., successfully withstood the whole of the 31st Japanese Division, until finally relieved by 2nd Division, in this subsidiary action.

The Honour was emblazoned by the:-
    Royal West Kent Regiment

RELIEF OF KOHIMA

5th to 20th April, 1944

In this subsidiary action, 2nd Division, with 161st Indian Brigade, carried out the operation to raise the siege of Kohima.

The Honour has been awarded to the:-
    Royal Scots   Cameron Highlanders
    Worcestershire Regiment

NAGA VILLAGE

4th May to 4th June, 1944

5th Brigade (2nd Division), and 7th Indian Division (less 89th Indian Brigade), were involved in this subsidiary action. The Japanese were holding out in the Naga village of Kohima, overlooking the rest of Kohima. 5th Brigade worked their way on to the north end of the ridge, and after severe fighting 7th Indian Division evicted the enemy.

The Honour has been awarded to the:-
    Lancashire Fusiliers   Cameron Highlanders
    Worcestershire Regiment

ARADURA

14th May to 6th June, 1944

In this subsidiary engagement, 2nd Division attacked the Japanese holding positions astride the main road to Imphal.

The Honour was emblazoned by the:-
    Royal Norfolk Regiment

and was also awarded to the:-
    Royal Scots   Cameron Highlanders

MAO SONGSANG

15th to 19th June, 1944

This subsidiary engagement was the last stand of the Japanese on the Kohima-Imphal road. 2nd Division and 114th Indian Brigade (7th Indian Division), were involved.

The Honour has been awarded to the:-
    Worcestershire Regiment   Royal Berkshire Regiment

UKHRUL

24th June to 20th July, 1944

In this Action, 33rd Indian, and 89th Indian Brigades, advanced direct on Ukhrul from the north and west, while 23rd Long Range Penetration Brigade cut the tracks between Ukhrul and the Chindwin to the east. 20th Indian Division (less 32nd Indian Brigade), closed in from the south-west. As a result, 15th and 31st Japanese Divisions were destroyed.

The Honour has been awarded to the:-

    Devonshire Regiment   Border Regiment
    King's Own Scottish Borderers.

TENGNOUPAL

21st to 28th July, 1944

In this Action, 23rd Indian Division drove the Japanese from the Shenam Pass. 268th Indian Lorried Infantry Brigade, and 5th Brigade (2nd Division), were also involved.

The Honour is borne on the Appointments of the:-

    10th Gurkha Rifles

and was also awarded to the:-

    Seaforth Highlanders

KENNEDY PEAK

3rd October to 7th November, 1944

In this Action, in which 5th Indian Division were involved, the Japanese rearguard, holding firmly to this dominating area, offered the most serious resistance during their retreat through the Chin Hills to the Chindwin.

The Honour is borne on the Standard of the:-

    3rd Dragoon Guards

MAWLAIK

28th October to 10th November, 1944

In this Engagement, 21st East African Brigade and 268th Indian Lorried Infantry Brigade, captured the river port of Mawlaik, and eliminated the Japanese bridgehead.

The Honour is borne on the Colours of the:-

    King's African Rifles

and was also awarded to the:-

    Northern Rhodesia Regiment

PINWE

11th to 30th November, 1944

In this Action, 36th Division cleared the valley through which the railway from Mogaung to Indaw and Katha runs. The first serious opposition was set at Pinwe, and the fighting continued for 20 day.

The Honour was emblazoned by the:-

    Royal Scots Fusiliers   East Lancashire Regiment
    South Wales Borderers
    Gloucestershire Regiment

and was also awarded to the:-

    Royal Sussex Regiment   Manchester Regiment

KALEWA

13th November to 16th December, 1944

In this Engagement, 11th East African Division captured the river port, and Japanese base at Kalewa, and established a bridgehead.

The Honour is borne on the Colours of the:-

    King's African Rifles   Northern Rhodesia Regiment

SHWEBO

6th to 9th January, 1945

This Action, in which 2nd Division, and elements of 19th Indian Division, took part, embraced fighting in a converging movement on Shwebo.

The Honour is borne on the Standard of the:-

    3rd Dragoon Guards

and was also awarded to the:-

    Royal Scots   Manchester Regiment
    Worcestershire Regiment   Cameron Highlanders
    Royal Berkshire Regiment   6th Gurkha Rifles

MONYWA, 1945

7th to 22nd January

20th Indian Division, in this Action, was opposed by Japanese rearguards resisting strongly.

The Honour was awarded to the:-

    Northamptonshire Regiment

SHWELI

1st January to 12th February, 1945

In this Engagement, 36th Division crossed the Irrawaddy and advanced south astride the Shweli river on Mogok. There was a stiff fight to cross the Shweli near Myitson.

The Honour was emblazoned by the:-

    Buffs

and was also awarded to the:-

Royal Scots Fusiliers	Royal Sussex Regiment
South Wales Borderers	
Gloucestershire Regiment	

KYAUKMYAUNG BRIDGEHEAD

9th January to 12th February, 1945

In this Action, 19th Indian Division seized the two bridgeheads of Thabeikkyin and Kyaukmyaung across the Irrawaddy, which the Japanese counter-attacked fiercely and unsuccessfully.

The Honour is borne on the Colours and Appointments of the:-

Welch Regiment	6th Gurkha Rifles

and was also awarded to the:-

    Royal Berkshire Regiment

SAGAING

23rd January to 12th February, 1945

In this Action, 2nd Division gradually disposed of a Japanese force left north of the Irrawaddy in the Sagaing area.

The Honour is borne on the Standard of the:-

    3rd Dragoon Guards

MANDALAY

12th/13th February to 21st March, 1945

In this Battle, XXXIII Corps captured Mandalay to link up with the Chinese forces, and thus secure the Burma-China road, and Air Ferry.

The Honour was emblazoned by the:-

3rd Dragoon Guards	Cameron Highlanders
Worcestershire Regiment	6th Gurkha Rifles
Dorset Regiment	10th Gurkha Rifles
Royal Berkshire Regiment	

and was also awarded to the:-

Royal Scots	Border Regiment
Royal Norfolk Regiment	Durham Light Infantry
Royal Scots Fusiliers	Royal Welch Fusiliers

MYITSON
13th February to 9th March, 1945

In this subsidiary action, 36th Division (26th, 29th and 72nd Brigades) had to fight hard to establish a firm bridgehead at Myitson, and then move on Mongmit. Under enveloping pressure, Japanese resistance finally broke.

The Honour is borne on the Colours of the:-

    Gloucestershire Regiment

and has also been awarded to the:-

    Buffs   South Wales Borderers

AVA
13th February to 20th March, 1945

In this subsidiary engagement, 2nd Division crossed the Irrawaddy west of Sagaing turned east along the south bank and took Ava, assisted by 268th Indian Lorried Infantry Brigade.

The Honour is borne on the Standard of the:-

    3rd Dragoon Guards

and was also awarded to the:-

    Cameron Highlanders   Royal Welch Fusliers

MYINMU BRIDGEHEAD
12th February to 7th March, 1945

This subsidiary action involved an opposed crossing of the Irrawaddy by 20th Indian Division, and fierce counter-attacks by the Japanese.

The Honour was emblazoned by the:-

    Devonshire Regiment   Northamptonshire Regiment
    Border Regiment   10th Gurkha Rifles

and was also awarded to the:-

    Manchester Regiment

FORT DUFFERIN
9th to 20th March, 1945

In this subsidiary action, in which the bulk of 19th Indian Division was involved, the Japanese fought to the death to hold Mandalay.

The Honour is borne on the Appointments of the:-

    6th Gurkha Rifles

and was also awarded to the:-

    Royal Berkshire Regiment

MAYMYO

11th to 12th March, 1945

62nd Indian Brigade Group (19th Indian Division) secured Maymyo in this subsidiary engagement, thereby covering the left flank of the attack on Mandalay.

The Honour was awarded to the:-

    Welch Regiment   6th Gurkha Rifles

SEIKPYU

10th to 16th February, 1945

In this Engagement, 28th East African Brigade made a feint crossing in connection with the Battle of Meiktila, the Enemy reacted strongly, and threw back the Brigade to Letse.

The Honour has been awarded to the:-

    King's African Rifles

KYAUKSE, 1945

8th to 31st March

In this Action, 20th Indian Division, breaking out from the Myinmu Bridgehead, advanced east to cut the road south of Mandalay.

The Honour has been awarded to the:-

    Devonshire Regiment   10th Gurkha Rifles

MEIKTILA

12th February to 30th March, 1945

In this Battle, IV Corps (5th Indian, 7th Indian and 17th Indian Divisions, and 255th Indian Tank Brigade), moved secretly down the Myittha Valley, forced a passage over the Irrawaddy at Nyaungu, and drove straight for Meiktila. An enemy counter-offensive was broken, and the enemy was pursued southwards by the IV and XXXIII Corps.

The Honour was emblazoned by the:-

    West Yorkshire Regiment   7th Gurkha Rifles
    Border Regiment   10th Gurkha Rifles

and was also awarded to the:-

    King's Own Scottish Borderers
    South Lancashire Regiment

NYAUNGU BRIDGEHEAD

12th to 21st February, 1945

7th Indian Division, in this subsidiary action, after sharp fighting at Kanhla and Pakokku, forced the Irrawaddy at Nyaungu, and held the bridgehead.

The Honour was emblazoned by the:-

    South Lancashire Regiment

CAPTURE OF MEIKTILA

28th February to 2nd March, 1945

In this subsidiary action, 17th Indian Division and 255th Indian Tank Brigade, stormed the town by infantry and armoured assault.

The Honour was awarded to the:-

    West Yorkshire Regiment   10th Gurkha Rifles
    7th Gurkha Rifles

DEFENCE OF MEIKTILA

3rd to 29th March, 1945

In this subsidiary action, the town was defended by 17th Indian Division, and 255th Indian Tank Brigade against a counter-attack by enemy infantry and armour.

The Honour was awarded to the:-

    West Yorkshire Regiment   10th Gurkha Rifles
    7th Gurkha Rifles

TAUNGTHA

24th February and 14th to 28th March, 1945

In this subsidiary engagement, in which 48th Indian Brigade (17th Indian Division), 255th Indian Tank Brigade, 161st Indian Brigade (5th Indian Division) and 33rd Indian Brigade (7th Indian Division) were concerned, the enemy were driven off this commanding point by 48th Indian Brigade. The enemy later retook it, only to lose it again.

The Honour was awarded to the:-

    Royal West Kent Regiment

LETSE

23rd February to 10th April, 1945

In this Engagement, 28th East African Brigade was attacked at Letse, where it had dug in after being driven back from Seikpyu. The situation became critical, and 114th Indian Brigade was drawn into the fighting.

The Honour has been awarded to the:-

    South Lancashire Regiment   King's African Rifles

IRRAWADDY

29th March to 30th May, 1945

This Battle, fought by XXXIII Corps, covers the fighting astride the Irrawaddy to destroy the 28th Japanese Army, which was trying to hold open a crossing over the river to enable its forces to the west of it, and from Arakan to escape.

The Honour is borne on the Standard, Colours and Appointments of the:-

    3rd Dragoon Guards   2nd Gurkha Rifles
    King's Own Scottish Borderers

and was also awarded to the:-

> Worcestershire Regiment
> South Lancashire Regiment
> Northamptonshire Regiment
> Manchester Regiment
> Cameron Highlanders
> 10th Gurkha Rifles

MT. POPA

2nd to 20th April, 1945

5th Brigade (2nd Division), and 268th Indian Lorried Infantry Brigade were involved in this subsidiary engagement, in which they cleared Mt. Popa in order to secure the flank and rear of 7th Indian Division, attacking the Yenangyaung Oilfields.

The Honour has been awarded to the:-

> Worcestershire Regiment
> Dorset Regiment
> Cameron Highlanders

YENANGYAUNG, 1945

18th to 25th April

In this subsidiary action, 7th Indian Division advanced astride the Irrawaddy to clear the Yenangyaung Oilfields. The action includes the fighting at Salin, west of the river, by 114th Indian Brigade, and that at Chauk and Kyaukpadaung by 89th and 33rd Indian Brigades, and 'Kingcol' of 7th Indian Division.

The Honour was awarded to the:-

> 3rd Dragoon Guards
> Queen's Royal Regiment

MAGWE

11th to 23rd April, 1945

In this subsidiary engagement, 20th Indian Division advanced from Meiktila to Magwe in order to cut the retreat of the Japanese forces holding the Yenangyaung oilfields.

The Honour was awarded to the:-

> 2nd Gurkha Rifles

KAMA

20th to 30th May, 1945

80th Indian Brigade (20th Indian Division), 33rd Indian Brigade (7th Indian Division) and 268th Indian Lorried Infantry Brigade were involved in this subsidiary action, when a considerable enemy force was trapped in the bridgehead after crossing the River Kama, and attempted to break out.

The Honour has been awarded to the:-

> King's Own Scottish Borderers

RANGOON ROAD

1st April to 6th May, 1945

In this Battle, IV Corps, with elements of 26th Indian Division under command, advanced to take Rangoon, after the collapse of the Japanese counter offensive against Meiktila. An amphibious and parachute assault on Rangoon by XV Corps, formed part of the operations.

The Honour is borne on the Appointments of the:-

    6th Gurkha Rifles   10th Gurkha Rifles
    7th Gurkha Rifles

and was also awarded to the:-

    West Yorkshire Regiment   Royal Berkshire Regiment
    Border Regiment   York and Lancaster Regiment
    Welch Regiment

PYAWBWE

1st to 10th April, 1945

In this subsidiary action, Pyawbwe was the centre of the line the enemy hoped to hold. The assault was made by 17th Indian Division (48th Indian, 63rd Indian and 116th Indian Brigades), with armoured support.

The Honour was awarded to the:-

    West Yorkshire Regiment   7th Gurkha Rifles
    Border Regiment

TOUNGOO

22nd April to 6th May, 1945

17th Indian, and 19th Indian Divisions, in this subsidiary engagement, moved swiftly to Toungoo to capture the airfields.

The Honour was awarded to the:-

    Royal Berkshire Regiment   6th Gurkha Rifles
    York and Lancaster Regiment

PEGU, 1945

27th April to 2nd May

In this subsidiary action, 17th Indian Div and 255th Indian Tank Brigade overcame a last Japanese effort to keep open the escape route to Mokpalin.

The Honour was awarded to the:-

    10th Gurkha Rifles

SITTANG, 1945

10th May to 15th August

In this Battle, fought by IV Corps (5th Indian, 7th Indian, 17th Indian, 19th Indian and 20th Indian Divisions), the Japanese 28th Army was cut off in the Pegu Yomas, while the remnants of their 33rd Army, on the east bank of the Sittang, attempted to keep open escape routes across the river. Much of the fighting included searching for small Japanese parties on a company basis.

The Honour was emblazoned by the:-

West Yorkshire Regiment	6th Gurkha Rifles
Welch Regiment	7th Gurkha Rifles (with 'Sittang, 1942')

and was also awarded to the:-

Queen's Royal Regiment	Royal West Kent Regiment
East Yorkshire Regiment	2nd Gurkha Rifles
Border Regiment	10th Gurkha Rifles

POINT 1433

8th to 12th September, 1944

This was a key point on the spine of the Mayu range. In this Engagement, assaults were made leading to its capture after fierce close fighting. 3/2 G.R., 17/5 Mahratta Regiment and 14/10 Baluch Regiment took part.

The Honour has been awarded to the:-

2nd Gurkha Rifles

TINMA

14th to 16th December, 1944

In this Engagement, the Japanese launched a fierce counter-attack against the 81st West African Division's base at Tinma. They were defeated with heavy loss.

The Honour has been awarded to the:-

Gold Coast Regiment

MAYU VALLEY

11th to 31st December, 1944

25th Indian Division, 82nd West African Division, and 50th Indian Tank Brigade took part in this Action, which was part of the operation to clear the Japanese from Arakan. 82nd Division had hard fighting north of Rathedaung.

The Honour has been awarded to the:-

Nigeria Regiment	Gold Coast Regiment

MYOHAUNG

15th to 25th January, 1945

81st West African and 82nd West African Divisions, (each less one brigade) fought this action. After the capture of Akyab Island, 81st Division met with stubborn opposition in its advance on Myohaung. With the support of two brigades from 82nd Division the town was secured, the Japanese having disintegrated and fled.

The Honour is borne on the Colours of the:-

Nigeria Regiment
Gold Coast Regiment
Sierra Leone Regiment

ARAKAN BEACHES

12th January to 29th April, 1945

This Battle involved 25th Indian, 26th Indian and 82nd West African Divisions, 3rd Commando Brigade and 50th Indian Tank Brigade. It was the closing operation of XV Corps in the campaign, and included cutting the Japanese communications by land and water to the Kaladan Valley, establishing an air supply base for Fourteenth Army on Ramree Island, and containing portions of two Japanese divisions on the coast as far as Taungup.

The Honour is borne on the Colours of the:-

King's African Rifles
Rhodesian African Rifles
Northern Rhodesia Regiment

and was also awarded to the:-

Green Howards
York and Lancaster Regiment
Oxfordshire and Buckinghamshire
   Light Infantry
2nd Gurkha Rifles
Nigerian Regiment
Gold Coast Regiment

MYEBON

12th to 21st January, 1945

This subsidiary action was undertaken to cut the Japanese water line of communication to the Kaladan Valley. 3rd Commando Brigade landed at the top of the Myebon peninsula, and after hard fighting were stopped south of Myebon. 74th Indian Brigade came into action on the 15th January, and by 18th, the whole enemy force was dead or dispersed.

The Honour has been awarded to the:-

2nd Gurkha Rifles
Commando Association

RAMREE

21st January to 15th February, 1945

In this subsidiary action, 26th Indian Division and 22nd East African Brigade captured Ramree and adjoining islands. Some determined opposition was met.

The Honour was awarded to the:-

Royal Lincolnshire Regiment

KANGAW

23rd January to 17th February, 1945

3rd Commando Brigade, 51st Indian Brigade, 74th Indian Brigade and 82nd West African Division were involved in this subsidiary action, which was successfully fought to cut the road Taungup – Myohaung. The enemy fought fiercely and desperately, but were either all killed or driven from their positions.

The Honour has been awarded to the:-

    Nigeria Regiment   Commando Association
    Gold Coast Regiment

DALET

27th February to 4th March, 1945

In this subsidiary engagement, 1st West African Brigade was strongly opposed on the Dalet Chaung, by enemy in commanding positions, while moving on An. The Brigade succeeded in crossing the Chaung, and securing the village.

The Honour is borne on the Colours of the:-

    Nigeria Regiment

TAMANDU

27th February to 11th March, 1945

In this subsidiary engagement, 74th Indian Brigade, passing through the Ru-Ywa bridgehead, drove the Japanese north of the Me Chaung. Enemy resistance then stiffened within half a mile of Tamandu. After a period of bitter fighting, the village was captured with the assistance of 4th West African Brigade coming from the north.

The Honour is borne on the Appointments of the:-

    2nd Gurkha Rifles

and was also awarded to the:-

    Oxfordshire and Buckinghamshire Light Infantry
    Nigeria Regiment

TAUNGUP

3rd to 29th April, 1945

This subsidiary engagement embraced holding the enemy in front of An with 22nd East African Brigade, while 4th Indian Brigade fought their way into Taungup.

The Honour is borne on the Colours of the:-

    Gold Coast Regiment   Rhodesian African Rifles
    Northern Rhodesia Regiment

and was also awarded to the:-

    King's African Rifles

CHINDITS, 1943

January to June

This Action covers the operations of 77th Indian Brigade in North Burma. The Brigade crossed the Chindwin river and the Mandalay-Myitkyina railway, and then the Irrawaddy. The following minor operations took place during the period: railway demolitions at Bonchaung and Nankan (6th March), ambushes at Pego-Sittang road (23rd March) and Baw (24th March), engagements at Hintha (28th March) and Okthaik (30th April).

The Honour was emblazoned by the:-
>King's Regiment

and was also awarded to the:-
>2nd Gurkha Rifles

CHINDITS, 1944

February to August

This Action involved 3rd Indian Division (16th Brigade, 77th Indian, 111th Indian, 14th British and 3rd West African, Brigades). The object was to disrupt the communications of the Japanese opposing General Stilwell. 77th Brigade established a firm block on the road and railway at Henu ('White City'), while 16th, 14th and 111th Brigades disrupted communications to south and west. 16th Brigade tried to capture (nearly successfully) the airfield at Indaw. Then 111th Brigade established a block at Hopin ('Blackpool') and 77th Brigade attacked and captured Mogaung. Other fighting occurred at 'Broadway' (the landing ground), Kyusanlai Pass, Point 2171 – Hill 60, and Myitkyina.

The Honour was emblazoned by the:-

King's Own Royal Regiment	Duke of Wellington's Regiment
King's Regiment	Border Regiment
Royal Leicestershire Regiment	South Staffordshire Regiment
Lancashire Fusiliers	Essex Regiment
Cameronians	York and Lancaster Regiment
Bedfordshire and Hertfordshire Regiment	6th Gurkha Rifles
	Nigeria Regiment

and was also awarded to the:-

Queen's Royal Regiment	Black Watch

HONORARY DISTINCTIONS

The following Honorary Distinctions were awarded to recognise the services during the Second World War of regiments and units which fought in an Arm, other than their own, to which Battle Honours are not customarily awarded. In these cases, the regiments and units were subsequently reconverted to a role in which they were once again entitled to carry Guidons or Colours.

THE SHROPSHIRE YEOMANRY
A Badge of the Royal Regiment or Artillery, with year-dates '1943-45' and two scrolls: 'Sicily,' 'Italy.'

THE AYRSHIRE YEOMANRY (EARL OF CARRICK'S OWN)
A Badge of the Royal Regiment of Artillery, with year-dates '1942-45' and three scrolls: 'North-West Europe,' 'North Africa,' 'Italy.'

THE CHESHIRE YEOMANRY (EARL OF CHESTER'S)
A Badge of the Royal Corps of Signals, with year-date '1945,' and one scroll: 'North-West Europe.'

THE LEICESTERSHIRE YEOMANRY (PRINCE ALBERT'S OWN)
A Badge of the Royal Regiment of Artillery, with year-dates '1942, '44-45,' and three scrolls: 'North-West Europe,' 'North Africa,' 'Sicily,' 'Italy.'

THE NORTH SOMERSET YEOMANRY
A Badge of the Royal Corps of Signals, with year-dates '1942-45,' and four scrolls: 'North-West Europe,' 'North Africa,' Sicily,' 'Italy.'

THE DUKE OF LANCASTER'S OWN YEOMANRY
A Badge of the Royal Regiment of Artillery, with year-dates '1942-45,' and two scrolls: 'North-West Europe,' 'Italy.'

THE LANARKSHIRE YEOMANRY
A Badge of the Royal Regiment of Artillery, with year-dates '1941-45,' and four scrolls: 'North-West Europe,' 'Sicily,' 'Italy,' 'Malaya.'

THE NORTHUMBERLAND HUSSARS
A Badge of the Royal Regiment of Artillery, with year-dates '1940-45,' and five scrolls: 'North-West Europe,' 'North Africa,' 'Greece,' 'Middle East,' 'Sicily.'

THE QUEEN'S OWN WORCESTERSHIRE HUSSARS
A Badge of the Royal Regiment of Artillery, with year-dates '1940, '44-45,' and one scroll: 'North-West Europe.'

THE QUEEN'S OWN ROYAL GLASGOW YEOMANRY
A Badge of the Royal Regiment of Artillery, with year-dates '1940, '44-45,' and four scrolls: 'North-Wet Europe,' 'North Africa,' 'Sicily,' 'Italy.'

THE SCOTTISH HORSE
A Badge of the Royal Regiment of Artillery, with year-dates '1943-45,' and three scrolls: 'North-West Europe,' 'Sicily,' 'Italy.'

THE CITY OF LONDON YEOMANRY (ROUGH RIDERS)
A Badge of the Royal Regiment of Artillery, with year-dates '1942-45,' and two scrolls: 'North Africa,' 'Italy.'

5TH BATTALION, THE KING'S OWN ROYAL REGIMENT (LANCASTER)
A Badge of the Royal Armoured Corps, with year-dates '1944-45,' and one scroll: 'North-West Europe.'

7TH (LEEDS RIFLES) BATTALION, THE WEST YORKSHIRE REGIMENT (THE PRINCE OF WALES'S OWN)
A Badge of the Royal Tank Regiment, with year-dates '1942-45,' and two scrolls: 'North Africa,' 'Italy.'

5TH BATTALION, THE GLOUCESTERSHIRE REGIMENT
A Badge of the Reconnaissance Corps, with year-dates '1944-45,' and one scroll: 'North-West Europe.'

5TH BATTALION, THE LOYAL REGIMENT (NORTH LANCASHIRE)
A Badge of the Reconnaissance Corps, with year-date '1942,' and one scroll: 'Malaya.'

17TH BATTALION, THE PARACHUTE REGIMENT
A Badge of the Durham Light Infantry, with year-dates '1940, '42-45' and three scrolls: 'North-West Europe,' 'North Africa,' 'Sicily.'

23RD LONDON REGIMENT
A Badge of the Royal Tank Regiment, with year-dates '1941-45,' and three scrolls: 'North-West Europe,' 'North Africa,' 'Italy.'

KOREA, 1950-53

This campaign was notable as being the first operation in which a United Nations force was formed and took part. Under American command, a British brigade took the field initially, expanding later into the 1st Commonwealth Division. The fighting units included British, Australian and Canadian battalions.

Thirty-one Battle Honours were named. Of these, some applied solely to Australian or Canadian units.

The Honour 'Korea, 1950-51,' is borne on the Colours of the:-

8th King's Royal Irish Hussars	Middlesex Regiment
Royal Northumberland Fusiliers	Royal Ulster Rifles
Gloucestershire Regiment	Argyll and Sutherland Highlanders

The Honour 'Korea, 1951-53' is borne on the Standards of the:-

Royal Tank Regiment

The Honour 'Korea, 1951-52,' is borne on the Colours of the:-

5th Royal Inniskilling Dragoon Guards	King's Own Scottish Borderers
Royal Norfolk Regiment	Welch Regiment
Royal Leicestershire Regiment	King's Shropshire Light Infantry

The Honour 'Korea, 1952-53,' is borne on the Colours of the:-

Royal Fusiliers	Black Watch
King's Regiment (Liverpool)	Durham Light Infantry
Duke of Wellington's Regiment (West Riding)	

NAKTONG BRIDGEHEAD

16th to 25th September, 1950

In this Battle, 8th U.S. Army launched an offensive against strong enemy opposition for a break out, from the Pusan perimeter, across the Naktong River. 27th British Infantry Brigade advanced on the 21st September, overcoming strong resistance, to enter Songju on the 26th September.

The Honour is borne on the Colours of the:-

Middlesex Regiment

CHONGJU

25th to 30th October, 1950

In this Engagement, 27th British Commonwealth Brigade (1/Mx., 1/A. & S.H., and 3/R.A.R.) acting as Advanced Guards to 24th U.S. Infantry Division, crossed the Chongchon river, and advanced north. 3/R.A.R. established a bridgehead and held it against enemy attacks. On the 26th October, 1/Mx. And 1/A. & S.H. crossed the Taeryong river at Pakchon to link up with 3/R.A.R., and next day 1/Mx. Successfully attacked an enemy rearguard, suffering 7 casualties, but inflicting on the enemy a loss of 10 tanks, 2 S.P. guns, 75 killed and 20 prisoners. On the following day, 3/R.A.R. and 1/A. & S.H. were closely engaged, and inflicted further heavy loss on the enemy.

The Honour has been awarded to the:-

Middlesex Regiment

PAKCHON

4th to 5th November, 1950

In this Engagement, strong enemy attacks against the Americans met with some success. Both 1/A&S.H. and 3/R.A.R. were called on for counter-attacks before the situation was restored, and heavy casualties were inflicted on the enemy.

The Honour is borne on the Colours of the:-
  Argyll and Sutherland Highlanders

CHONGCHON II

25th to 30th November, 1950

This was an American Battle, during which 1/Mx. Became involved in some sharp fighting in conjunction with American troops.

The Honour has been awarded to the:-
  Middlesex Regiment

SEOUL

2nd to 4th January, 1951

This was an American Battle, during which 29th British Infantry Brigade Group (under command of I U.S. Corps) was heavily attacked. The Brigade occupied a defensive position North-West of Seoul, in the vicinity of Chungchung-Dong. The enemy attacked and, after being driven back by local counter-attacks, the Brigade withdrew fighting to south of the River Han.

The Honour has been awarded to the:-

8th King's Royal Irish Hussars	Royal Ulster Rifles
Royal Northumberland Fusiliers	

CHAUM-NI

14th to 17th February, 1951

During this Engagement, 27th British Commonwealth Brigade, under command of 2nd U.S. Division, carried out a successful advance along the road Tangu-Ri-Chipyong-Ni, during which some heavy fighting took place.

The Honour was awarded to the:-
  Middlesex Regiment

HILL 327

16th to 20th February, 1951

In this Engagement, 29th British Infantry Brigade Group came under command of 25th U.S. Division, in the Kyongan-Ni area. It took part in the successful attack to gain the 'Boston' line.

The Honour has been awarded to the:-
  Gloucestershire Regiment   8th King's Royal Irish Hussars

KAPYONG-CHON
3rd to 16th April, 1951

27th British Commonwealth Brigade fought this Engagement under command of IX U.S. Corps during the advance against enemy rearguards, to capture the 'Kansas' line.

The Honour was awarded to the:-

    Middlesex Regiment

IMJIN
22nd to 25th April, 1951

This Engagement took place on the launching of a major Chinese offensive against the United Nations. 29th British Infantry Brigade Group held the left sector of 3rd U.S. Division on the river Imjin. All units of the Brigade had heavy fighting until it withdrew on the 25th April.

The Honour was emblazoned on the Guidon and Colours of the:-

    8th King's Royal Irish Hussars   Gloucestershire Regiment
    Royal Northumberland Fusiliers   Royal Ulster Rifles

KAPYONG
22nd to 25th April, 1951

In this Engagement, 27th British Commonwealth Brigade, as a result of enemy penetration in IX U.S. Corps area, occupied blocking positions, and after constant enemy attacks finally compelled the enemy to withdraw.

The Honour was awarded to the:-

    Middlesex Regiment

KOWANG-SAN
3rd to 12th October, 1951

This Action, which was an operation carried out by I U.S. Corps, entailed an advance against enemy opposition between Changdan and the North-East of Chorwon. The British Commonwealth Division attacked between the Rivers Samichon and Imjin.

The Honour is borne on the Colours of the:-

    King's Own Scottish Borderers   King's Shropshire Light Infantry

and was also awarded to the:-

    Royal Northumberland Fusiliers   8th King's Royal Irish Horses

MARYANG-SAN
4th to 6th November, 1951

A strong attack on the 28th British Commonwealth Infantry Brigade in this Engagement led to heavy fighting, particularly for 1/K.O.S.B. and 1/K.S.L.I 1/R. Leics. Became involved on the 5th November in heavy fighting to restore the situation.

The Honour has been awarded to the:-

  Royal Leicestershire Regiment   King's Own Scottish Borderers

HILL 227 I
17th to 19th November, 1951

In this Engagement, 1/K.S.L.I. bore the brunt of an enemy attack on 28th British Commonwealth Infantry Brigade.

The Honour has been awarded to the:-

  King's Shropshire Light Infantry

THE HOOK, 1952
18th to 19th November, 1952

In this Engagement, 29th British Infantry Brigade held the left sector of the Division astride the river Samichon. During an enemy attack, 1/B.W. after stiff fighting were forced back, but restored their position the next morning by counter-attack.

The Honour is borne on the Standard and Colours of the:-

  5th Royal Inniskilling Dragoon Guards   Black Watch

THE HOOK, 1953
28th to 29th May, 1953

In this Engagement, 29th British Infantry Brigade was holding the left sector of the Division astride the river Samichon. After heavy bombardment the enemy attacked and captured part of the position, which was successfully counter-attacked next day, re-establishing the position.

The Honour is borne on the Colours of the:-

  King's Regiment (Liverpool)   Duke of Wellington's Regiment

INDEX TO BATTLE HONOURS OF THE SECOND WORLD WAR (1939-45) AND KOREA (1950-53)

A

Aam	31
Aart	26
Abyssinia, 1940-41, 1942	42
Adrano	96
Adriatic	141
Ad Teclesan	45
Advance on Tripoli	72
Advance to Florence	116
Advance to Tiber	113
Afodu	46
Agedabia	60
Agira	95
Agordat	43
Akarit	75
Alam el Halfa	70
Alem Hamza	63
Alessandra	48
Alethangyaw	153
Aller	39
Amba Alagi	45
Ambazzo	51
Amiens, 1940	6
Amiens, 1944	24
Ancona	120
Antwerp	25
Antwerp-Turnhout Canal	28
Anzio	109
Aprilia	109
Aquino	112
Aradura	157
Arakan Beaches	167
Arezzo	116
Argenta Gap	134
Argoub el Megas	90
Argoub Sellah	87
Arnhem, 1944	27
Arnhem, 1945	41
Arras counter attack	6
Artlenberg	41
Asten (or Meijel)	31
Athens	138
Augusta	94
Ava	161
Awash	49

B

Babile Gap	48
Baghdad, 1941	53
Banana Ridge	86
Bardia, 1941	59
Barentu	43
Barkasan	52
Battaglia	131
Battipaglia	103
Batu Pahat	145
Beda Fomm	59
Beles Gugani	47
Belhamed	63
Benghazi	64
Benghazi Raid	71
Bentheim	39
Ber Rabal	87
Best	27
Bir el Aslagh	65
Bir el Igela	65
Bir Enba	58
Bir Hacheim	66
Bishenpur	156
Bisidimo	49
Bologna	135
Bordj	85

176

Bou Arada	79
Bou Ficha	92
Boulogne, 1940	6
Boulogne, 1944	28
Bourguebus Ridge	17
Bremen	40
Breville	13
Brieux Bridgehead	20
Brinkum	40
British Somaliland, 1940	52
Bruneval	10
Brussels	24
Bulo Erillo	47
Buq Buq	59
Burma, 1942-45	147, 148
Buthidaung	152

C

Caen	15
Cagny	18
Calabritto	106
Calais, 1940	7
Calais, 1944	28
Caldari	102
Cambes	12
Campoleone	109
Campriano	119
Canea	140
Cappezano	104
Capture of Forli	125
Capture of Halfaya Pass, 1942	72
Capture of Meiktila	163
Capture of Naples	104
Capture of Perugia	114
Capture of Ravenna	130
Capture of Tobruk	59
Cardito	105
Carmusa	64
Carpineta	124
Carroceto	110
Casa Bettini	126
Casa Fabbri Ridge	128
Casa Fortis	125
Casa Sinagogga	112
Cassel	8

Cassino I	110
Cassino II	111
Castle Hill	110
Catarelto Ridge	133
Catheolles	20
Cauldron	66
Cava di Tirreni	104
Central Malaya	144
Centuripe	96
Cerasola	108
Ceriano Ridge	128
Cesena	129
Chebket en Nouiges	76
Cheux	15
Chindits, 1943	169
Chindits, 1944	169
Chongchon II	173
Chongju	172
Chor es Sufan	63
Chaum-Ni	173
Citerna	119
Citta della Pieve	114
Citta di Castello	118
Cleve	35
Colito	49
Colle Cedro	107
Conventello-Comacchio	130
Coriano	121
Corinth Canal	138
Cos	141
Cosina Canal Crossing	125
Crete	139
Creteville Pass	92
Croce	122
Cubcub	44

D

Dalet	168
Damiano	108
Defence of Alamein Line	68
Defence of Arras	6
Defence of Escaut	5
Defence of Habbaniya	53
Defence of Kohima	157
Defence of Lamone Bridgehead	126

Defence of Meiktila	163
Defence of Rauray	15
Defence of Sinzweya	154
Defence of Tobruk	60
Deir el Munassib	71
Deir el Shein	69
Deir ez Zor	55
Derna Aerodrome	60
Dieppe	11
Dives Crossing	22
Djebel Abiod	77
Djebel Alliliga	80
Djebel Ang	86
Djebel Azzag, 1942	78
Djebel Azzag, 1943	79
Djebel Bech Chekaoui	85
Djebel Bel Mahdi	85
Djebel Bou Aoukaz, 1943, I	89
Djebel Bou Aoukaz, 1943, II	91
Djebel Choucha	83
Djebel Dahra	83
Djebel Djaffa	81
Djebel Djaffa Pass	87
Djebel el Meida	75
Djebel el Rhorab	84
Djebel el Telil	76
Djebel Garci	77
Djebel Guerba	82
Djebel Kesskiss	86
Djebel Kournine	90
Djebel Rmel	86
Djebel Roumana	76
Djebel Tanngoucha	86
Djebel Tebaga	77
Djedeida	78
Donbaik	150
Dreirwalde	39
Dunkirk, 1940	8
Dyle	5

E

Egyptian Frontier, 1940	58
El Agheila	72
El Alamein	71
El Hadjeba	81
El Hamma	74
El Kourzia	87
El Wak	46
Enfidaville	76
Esquay	17
Estry	21

F

Falaise	21
Falaise Road	22
Falluja	53
Ficulle	114
Fiesole	119
Fike	49
Filo	134
Flushing	30
Fondouk	83
Fondouk Pass	84
Fontenay le Pesnil	14
Foret de Bretonne	24
Foret de Nieppe	8
Fort Dufferin	161
Fort McGregor	81
Fossa Cembalina	135
Fossacesia	101
Francofonte	94
French Frontier, 1940	7
Frisoni	128
Fuka	68
Fuka Airfield	69

G

Gabbiano	116
Gab Gab Gap	89
Gabr el Fachri	67
Gabr Saleh	61
Gaiana Crossing	136
Gambela	46
Garigliano Crossing	107
Gazala	64
Geilenkirchen	32
Gelib	48
Gemmano Ridge	123

Gerbini	95
Gheel	25
Giarso	50
Gogni	48
Goluin	48
Gondar	51
Gothic Line	120
Greece, 1941, '44-45	137
Grich el Oued	88
Grik Road	143
Gromballa	92
Gubi I	61
Gubi II	63
Gueriat el Atach Ridge	88

H

Hagiag er Raml	66
Halfaya, 1941	60
Hammam Lif	91
Hangman's Hill	111
Hechtel	25
Heidous	86
Heppen	25
Heraklion	140
Hill 112	16
Hill 227 I	175
Hill 327	173
Hitler Line	112
Hochwald	36
Hong Kong	146
Honorary Distinctions	170
Hook, 1952, The	175
Hook, 1953, The	175
Htizwe	150
Hunt's Gap	82

I

Ibbenburen	38
Idice Bridgehead	136
Imjin	174
Imphal	154
Impossible Bridge	102
Incontro	118

Ipoh	144
Iraq, 1941	53
Irrawaddy	163
Italy, 1943-45	98, 99

J

Jebel Dafeis	42
Jebel Mazar	55
Jebel Shiba	43
Jitra	143
Johore	144
Juba	47
Jurques	19

K

Kairouan	84
Kaladan	152
Kalewa	159
Kama	164
Kampar	144
Kangaw	168
Kanglatongbi	156
Kapyong	174
Kapyong-chon	174
Karora-Marsa Taclai	44
Kasserine	80
Kef el Debna	83
Kef Ouiba Pass	82
Kennedy Peak	158
Keren	44
Knightsbridge	66
Kohima	156
Korea 1950-53	172
Kowang-San	174
Kulkaber	51
Kvam	1
Kyaukmyaung Bridgehead	160
Kyaukse, 1942	149
Kyaukse, 1945	162

L

Laison	22
Lamone Crossing	126
Landing at Porto San Venere	99
Landing in Sicily	93
La Touques Crossing	23
La Variniere	18
La Vie Crossing	23
Lechemti	50
Leese	39
Le Havre	28
Lentini	94
Le Perier Ridge	20
Leros	141
Letse	163
Lingen	38
Liri Valley	112
Lisiuex	23
Litan	155
Litani	54
Longstop Hill, 1942	79
Longstop Hill, 1943	88
Lower Maas	30

M

Madagascar	140
Magwe	164
Maknassy	83
Malaya, 1941-42	143
Malleto	97
Malta, 1940-1942	142
Maltot	18
Mandalay	160
Mao Songsan	157
Marda Pass	48
Mareth	73
Marradi	130
Maryang-San	175
Massa Tambourini	111
Massa Vertecchi	111
Massawa	45
Matmata Hills	75
Maungdaw	153
Mawlaik	158
Maymyo	162
Mayu Tunnels	153
Mayu Valley	166
Medenine	73
Medicina	136
Medjez el Bab	78
Medjez Plain	88
Meijel	31
Meiktila	162
Melfa Crossing	112
Menate	134
Mergueb Chaouach	85
Merjayun	54
Mersa el Brega	59
Mersa Matruh	67
Merville Battery	12
Mescelit Pass	44
Middle East, 1941-44	139
Mine de Sedjenane	83
Minqar Qaim	68
Minturno	107
Monastery Hill	110
Montagne Farm	82
Montarnaud	91
Montebello-Scorticata Ridge	123
Monte Camino	106
Monte Casalino	131
Monte Cavallo	125
Monte Ceco	131
Monte Cedrone	118
Monte Chicco	124
Monte Colombo	128
Monte Domini	117
Monte Farneto	124
Monte Gabbione	114
Monte Gamberaldi	130
Montegaudio	121
Monte Grande	132
Monte Gridolfo	121
Monte La Pieve	131
Monte Malbe	115
Monte Maro	105
Monte Ornito	108
Monte Pianoereno	131
Monte Piccolo	113
Monte Reggiano	123

Monte Rivoglia	97
Monte Rotondo	114
Monte San Michele	117
Monte Scalari	117
Montescudo	128
Monte Spaduro	132
Monte Stella	104
Monte Tuga	108
Montilgallo	124
Montone	118
Montorsoli	119
Mont Pincon	18
Monywa, 1942	18
Monywa, 1945	150
Mt. Engiahat	45
Mt. Popa	164
Mowdok	153
Moyale	46
Moyland and Moyland Wood	46
Mozzagrogna	101
Msus	64
Muar	145
Myebon	167
Myinmu Bridgehead	161
Myitson	161
Myohaung	167

N

Naga Village	157
Nakton Bridgehead	172
Nederrijn	26
Neerpelt	26
Ngakyedauk Pass	154
Nijmegen	27
Nofilia	72
Noireau Crossing	21
Normandy Landing	11
North Africa, 1940-43	56, 57
North Arakan	51
North Malaya	143
North-West Europe, 1940, 1942, 1944, 1945	3, 4
Norway, 1940	1, 2
Norway, 1941	2
Noyers	17

Nunshigum	155
Nyaungu Bridgehead	162

O

Odon	14
Omars	62
Omo	50
Opheusden	31
Orne	16
Orsara	132
Orsogna	102
Otta	1
Oudna	78
Oued Zarga	85
Ourthe	33

P

Pakchon	173
Palmyra	55
Paungde	149
Pegasus Bridge	11
Pegu, 1942	148
Pegu, 1945	165
Pergola Ridge	127
Peters Corner	89
Pian di Maggio	118
Pian di Castello	122
Pichon	84
Pideura	126
Pinwe	159
Poggio del Grillo	119
Poggio San Giovanni	122
Point 93	70
Point 174	68
Point 201 (Roman Wall)	74
Point 201 (Arakan)	151
Point 551	152
Point 1433	166
Port en Bessin	12
Pothus	2
Primosole Bridge	94
Proasteion	138
Pursuit to Messina	97

Putot en Bessin	123
Pyawbwe	165

Q

Quarry Hill	19

R

Ragoubet Souissi	91
Ramree	167
Rangoon Road	165
Rathedaung	150
Razabil	152
Regalbuto	96
Reichswald	35
Relief of Kohima	157
Relief of Tobruk	63
Retimo	140
Retma	65
Rhine	37
Rhineland	34
Rimini Line	127
Ripa Ridge	115
Risle Crossing	23
Robaa Valley	80
Rocchetta e Croce	106
Roer	33
Romagnoli	101
Rome	113
Ruweisat	69
Ruweisat Ridge	70

S

Saar	10
Sagain	160
Sakawng	155
Salerno	102
Salerno Hills	103
Salso Crossing	97
San Clemente	122
Sanfatucchio	115
Sangro	101
San Marino	129
San Martino Sogliano	124
San Nicolo Canal	135
San Salvo	100
Santarcangelo	123
Santa Lucia	103
Santerno Crossing	134
Saunnu	64
Savignano	124
Savio Bridgehead	129
Sbiba	80
Scafati Bridge	105
Schaddenhof	37
Scheldt	29
Sebkret en Noual	76
Sedjenane I	82
Seikpyu	162
Seine, 1944	24
Senio	133
Senio Floodbank	127
Senio Pocket	127
Seoul	173
Sferro	95
Sferro Hills	96
Shenam Pass	155
Shwebo	159
Shwegyin	150
Shweli	160
Si Abdallah	89
Sicily, 1943	93
Sidi Ahmed	90
Sidi Ali	84
Sidi Barrani	58
Sidi Nsir	81
Sidi Rezegh, 1941	62
Sidi Rezegh, 1942	67
Sidi Suleiman	60
Sillaro Crossing	136
Si Mediene	89
Simeto Bridgehead	95
Simeto Crossing	97
Singapore Island	145
Sittang, 1942	148
Sittang, 1945	166
Slim River	144
Solarino	94
Somme, 1940	9

Soroppa	47
Soudia	77
Souleuvre	20
South Beveland	29
South-East Asia, 1941	146
Southern France	41
Steamroller Farm	81
Stien	2
St Nazaire	10
St Omer-La Bassee	7
St Pierre La Vieille	21
Stuka Farm	81
St Valery-en-Caux	10
Sully	12
Syria, 1941	54

T

Taieb el Essem	62
Tadjera Khir	73
Takrouna	77
Tamandu	168
Tamera	82
Tamu Road	155
Taranto	100
Taukyan	149
Taungtha	163
Taungup	168
Tavoleto	121
Teano	106
Tebaga Gap	74
Tebourba	78
Tebourba Gap	78
Tengnoupal	158
Termoli	100
Thala	80
Tilly sur Seulles	13
Tinma	166
Tobruk, 1941	61
Tobruk, 1942	67
Tobruk Sortie, 1941	62
Todenyang-Namaraputh	47
Tossignano	132
Toungoo	165
Tourmauville Bridge	15
Traghetto	136

Trasimene Line	115
Trigno	100
Troarn	18
Tug Argan	52
Tuitum	154
Tunis	90
Tuori	116
Two Tree Hill	79

U

Uelzen	40
Ukhrul	158

V

Vaagso	2
Valli di Commachio	133
Veghel	27
Venlo Pocket	32
Venraij	31
Veve	137
Via Balbia	67
Vietri Pass	103
Villa Grande	102
Villers Bocage	13
Vist	1
Vizzini	94
Volturno Crossing	105

W

Waal Flats	35
Wadara	50
Wadi Akarit East	76
Wadi Zeuss East	74
Wadi Zigzaou	74
Walcheren Causeway	29
Wal Garis	46
Weeze	36
Westkapelle	30
West Point 23	70
Withdrawal to Cherbourg	10
Withdrawal to Escaut	5

Withdrawal to Matruh	58	Yenangyaung, 1945	164
Withdrawal to Seine	9	Ypres-Comines Canal	8
Withdrawal to Sphakia	140	Yu	151
Wormhoudt	7		

X

Xanten   37

Y

Yenangyaung, 1942   149

Z

Zemlet el Lebene	73
Zetten	33
Zt el Mrasses	67

www.ingramcontent.com/pod-product-compliance
Lightning Source LLC
Chambersburg PA
CBHW080550230426
43663CB00015B/2782